"*Wolf Girl* is much more than a coming-of-age story. It is an inspiring story of how one can overcome adversity, connect with nature, pursue their passion, follow synchronicity and discover a life filled with purpose and meaning. As a father of two teen girls, I believe these are the types of stories that are essential for our young people to read. Doniga is an amazing role model whose story will give teens hope and inspire them to become the next generation of nature-connected leaders and stewards that our world desperately needs."

—Warren Moon, Executive Director, Wilderness Awareness School

"With prose good enough to be called poetry, she brings us on a deeply moving and profound journey of awakening and awareness."

—Joel Salatin, farmer, lecturer, and author of *Folks, This Ain't Normal, You Can Farm, and Salad Bar Beef*

"*Wolf Girl* is a delicate balance of thrilling narrative and meditative reflection that echoes the precious ecological balances Doniga Markegard comes to understand as a teenager and later mimics as an adult on a regenerative ranch. As Markegard learns to track animals, she also tracks the edges of her humanity and spirituality in relation to the natural world. Reminiscent of Annie Dillard's *Pilgrim at Tinker Creek*, *Wolf Girl* is a tale of environmental awakening that will inspire the same curiosity, wonder, and back-to-the-land perspective in readers searching for meaning and avenues to action in a time of ecological chaos."

—Stephanie Anderson, author of *One Size Fits None: A Farm Girl's Search for the Promise of Regenerative Agriculture*

"This poignant and moving call to humans to reconnect with nature is a book for our times. While it is written for young adults—that increasingly activist generation who seek to clean up the mess of we previous generations—it will have a far wider appeal. This book deserves to be a bestseller."

—Charles Massy, author of *Call of the Reed Warbler*

"Doniga Markegard's journey from teen runaway to expert tracker and on to mother, rancher, and activist artfully conveys what it means to be fully alive to the natural world. In *Wolf Girl*, she sets out a path for readers seeking grounding and direction during a confusing time. Written with love and hard-won insight, this book is as inspiring as it is beautiful."

—Judith D. Schwartz, author of *Cows Save the Planet: And Other Improbable Ways of Restoring Soil to Heal the Earth*

"Doniga Markegard's remarkable and highly unconventional journey from a teenager badly out-of-sync with her world to a rancher and mother working closely with nature is an inspiring story about finding your purpose in life. In an era of gloomy news and uncertain visions of the future, Doniga's book is a breath of fresh, joyous air!"

—Courtney White, author of *Grass, Soil, Hope* and co-founder of the Quivira Coalition

"A wonderful book that shines a light on an exciting path that will inspire many."

—Tristan Gooley, author of *The Natural Navigator, The Lost Art of Reading Nature's Signs*, and *The Nature Instinct*

Wolf Girl

FINDING MYSELF IN THE WILD

Doniga Markegard

PROPRIOMETRICS
PRESS

Printed in the United States of America
First Printing 2020
ISBN-13: 9781943370184
Library of Congress Control Number: 2019955173

Propriometrics Press: propriometricspress.com
Cover and Interior Design: Zsofi Koller, liltcreative.co
Cover images: Musjaka, Shutterstock; Kate Macate, Creative Market
Author photo: Lee Foster

Library of Congress Cataloging-in-Publication Data
Names: Markegard, Doniga, author.
Title: Wolf Girl : finding myself in the wild / Doniga Markegard.
Description: First Edition. | Sequim, Washington : Propriometrics Press, 2020. | "Wilderenss Awareness School"--Cover. | Includes bibliographical
references and index. | Audience: Ages 14 years and up | Audience: Grades 10-12
Identifiers: LCCN 2019053779 (print) | LCCN 2019053780 (ebook) | ISBN
9781943370184 (Paperback) | ISBN 9781943370191 (eBook)
Subjects: LCSH: Markegard, Doniga--Juvenile literature. | Environmentalists--United States--Biography--Juvenile literature. | Women environmentalists--United States--Biography--Juvenile literature.
| Organic farmers--United States--Biography--Juvenile literature. | Wilderness survival--Juvenile literature. | Wolves--Juvenile literature.
Classification: LCC GE55 .M37 2020 (print) | LCC GE55 (ebook) | DDC
636/.01092 [B]--dc23
LC record available at https://lccn.loc.gov/2019053779
LC ebook record available at https://lccn.loc.gov/2019053780

For my daughters and all daughters who follow their passions and seek an adventurous path.

Contents

Preface ix

PART ONE

Chapter One: Trapped 2

Chapter Two: Freedom 14

Chapter Three: Calling.. 22

Chapter Four: Awareness 34

Five tracking tips to take wherever you go,
even your own backyard 58

Chapter Five: Language of Nature....................... 62

Chapter Six: Lone Wolf 77

Chapter Seven: Pack 88

Three things we can all learn from wolves 111

Chapter Eight: Vision 114

PART TWO

Chapter Nine: Food 144

Chapter Ten: Permaculture................................. 168

Easy ways to start eating like a regenetarian 182

Chapter Eleven: Home 185

Chapter Twelve: Family 220
   Three things you can track almost anywhere 230
Chapter Thirteen: Fire 233

Epilogue 243

References 247
Acknowledgments 252
About the Author 254

Preface

It's hard to be a young person right now. The climate crisis is picking up speed and creating terrible, terrifying changes. Wildfires are sweeping across huge areas, drought is threatening populated regions, flooding is ruining homes in other places. It's too hot, and our oceans are full of plastic. When we're teenagers we're taught to look to the future, but what future can you look to when the present is so bleak? Where can we find hope? How can we fix this mess?

I've been there. I felt overwhelmed and hopeless as a teenager. I could see that our way of life was destroying the planet I love, and I couldn't figure out how to be part of the solution. Nothing I tried seemed like enough.

But in time, I learned how to be a part of the solution every single day, by modeling my life and my career on the lessons I have learned from nature. You may see yourself in this story. It is a story that is close to many of us, that speaks to our intuition.

Wolf Girl is the story of my awakening as a teenager, so named because the wolf has guided me on my life's journey, often quite literally. This is the story of me coming of age, not only to separate myself from my family, but also to recognize my part in the web of life and see my role in reversing the environmental devastation caused by centuries of damaging industrial and agricultural practices. This is the story of what the wild has taught me, and how it can save us all.

When you're a teenager, it can be hard to see how your life is going to unfold before you. It's hard to know how your choices now can lead to the life you'll have in your twenties, thirties, and beyond.

But looking back, I can see so clearly how I got to where I am, where the wolves led me. I'm living a life where I am in tune with nature, where my work every day involves storing carbon back into the soil where it belongs. I'm feeding my community healthy food and creating lush, thriving land in a drought-ridden place. I'm a wolf girl, grown up: tending to my pack, playing my part in the health of the grasslands, and raising more wolf cubs.

The choices you make right now matter, and will continue to shape your life and the life of the planet. You can make those choices based on what you learn from the wilderness; it's talking to you right now. All you need to do is listen.

Part One

Trapped

CHAPTER ONE

I vowed to live my life free of regret when I awoke from unconsciousness at age thirteen.

I came to in the back seat of our rusty old Chevy truck. I rubbed my pounding head and looked down at my wrist to see a plastic hospital band bearing my name and phone number. I looked up at my mother sitting in the front seat. "What happened?" I said. "Where am I? I feel so confused."

"Sundance spooked at a ground hornet nest and threw you off when you were warming up for show jumping," my mother replied in a monotonous tone. She had clearly told me this over and over again. "They rushed you to the hospital. You need to get a lot of rest. You got a pretty bad concussion. I have been worried sick about you."

I was disoriented. Where was my horse? Had I let down my team? This was the one thing that meant the world to me. I was a girl with a horse. I woke up every morning to care for Sundance before school. My thoughts wandered throughout the day toward the next horse show or trail ride. I had what so many thirteen-year-old girls could only dream of: a horse in my front yard and limitless wilderness to ride. Now an entire section of my life had just disappeared from memory. I did not remember the ambulance ride or the events that led up to the fall. I had gone somewhere else, but where? My body was still here. I sat silently for a long time before I finally spoke.

"Mom, where was I when my body was lying in the hospital bed?" During the long drive home I told her what I could remember. The rain started to fall on the windshield and the rhythmic sound of the wipers kept me from drifting off into my thoughts. "I remember soaring over my body. I looked around at people I didn't recognize. Then I looked behind me. Everything around me disappeared—no people, no fluorescent hospital lights or machines." I described the abyss of darkness to my mother, and how when I looked closer I saw a passageway with a soft light at the other end. The light had been so inviting. It was soft like the dawn light when there are no clouds in the sky and the sun has not yet pierced the horizon. It was like the pure, clear light of the full moon. I told my mother I had been drawn to go through that dark passage toward the light. "It was like there was something I had been looking for in that light. It was…peaceful." I paused.

My heart longed to see that place through the passage. When I was soaring over my body I was in a realm between life and something else. It was not a place or a thing, but a feeling so awe-inspiring that words only detracted from the sheer brilliance. I held on to that moment. I had never experienced anything like it.

I had been soaring, my mind had no thoughts, and my body had no separation between the flesh and the universe surrounding me. I felt the sheer ecstasy of freedom from the burdens of my body, the imperfections of my life. All the complications of a teenage girl had volatized in that one moment.

I continued recounting my experience, shifting on the cracked vinyl seat, trying to find a position that soothed the pain in my head. "I looked behind me and I saw my body lying on the hospital bed. You were sitting next to me, Mom, with your hand on my shoulder. I could hear myself talking, but I was not making any sense. I was asking about Rebecca. Why was I asking about Rebecca?"

Mom spoke quietly. "She was the last person you talked to before your…" She paused. "Accident."

"Where is my team? Where is Emily?" I replied, anxious. "Did we win the blue ribbon? We were in the lead!"

"Emily wasn't on your team for this event," Mom said, scraping her thumbnail over the grimy steering wheel.

"Yes she was!" I cried out. "I was in the barn with her, cleaning the stalls before I…" But I trailed off, giving up, not sure of my recollection of the events.

Everything was so confusing; I had experienced a different reality. I couldn't differentiate between what was real and what was just a story that my mind had constructed. The only thing that seemed real to me was the euphoria I'd felt when I was soaring over my body. This accident ignited a search within me.

What had my physical body truly experienced after my fall? Why was my interpretation of the events that led up to my accident so different from my mother's? I was at a horse show, and the people and the events were similar to my mother's version of the story, but my recollection was unmistakably different. I could not remember what had happened in the days leading up to the show. When I was soaring over my body, I felt I could have gone into that passage toward the inviting soft light. So why hadn't I? Why had I come back into myself, the body lying on a hospital bed? If I had not come back, where would I be? Would I be living in a dreamland if I had gone toward that light? If I had not come back to my body, would the intellectual burdens of my brain no longer tie me down? Now that I was back here, how could I live a life that let me experience that rapture?

I had already begun questioning everything around me on the first day of seventh grade, the year before my horse accident.

That morning, I sat silent on a rock. The boulder jutted out of a vast concrete entryway next to the front parking lot of Chief Kanim Middle School. The school rose up from the concrete, a low, sprawling two-story building with tiny windows. Small poplar trees thrust up out of small holes chiseled into the concrete next to the entrance.

The school was brand new, and my Fall City, Washington, community was proud of it. But I felt differently. Before the school was built, this land had been a beautiful cedar forest with a large meadow, where I would often see deer grazing. I felt out of place in the building surrounded by concrete. I liked the elementary school I had attended the year before. It was an old brick building built in 1909. Through its large windows I could see into the courtyards that surrounded the school. The rhododendrons would bloom in March, signifying the transition from winter to spring and letting us know that summer break was just around the corner. I often watched the robins perch on those shrubs outside the classroom windows, hearing their muffled calls through the closed panes.

In elementary school we had been allowed to be kids. To get to some of our classes, we walked outside along the edge of a large meadow with trees all around it. I had my favorite cottonwood trees; I would play around their trunks during recess. The smell of the cottonwood buds as they burst open in the early spring on the first warm days was a celebration of the winter past. The reddish resin that dripped from their buds filled the air with the sweet smell of freshly cut pine infused with honey. My friends and I had a whole world of our own on that playground.

Now I was sitting on a cold, uncomfortable rock in the

middle of a sea of concrete. All of the kids around me were walking or talking and laughing in small groups. The only thing I could think about was getting out of school at the end of the day.

I entered the school when the bell rang. As I looked around my first class, I saw that the kids in the room were either stone cold bored or self-involved, busily trying to catch a glimpse from a classmate. I sat and did my math problems. The teacher, a thin older man with glasses, commented that he had never seen a girl with such a logical mind. What did that mean? I wondered at that moment if I should be more like the other girls in the class, fixing their hair, looking in their pocket mirrors to see if their makeup had smudged. I just sat silently, not knowing how to respond.

As the days went by, I became increasingly disillusioned with middle school. I was not interested in the things we were learning, and my teachers did not seem genuinely interested in the passions of the students. Just as I was hoping for a way out of school, I walked into my history class. There was a life-sized cutout poster of John Wayne up on the wall. His cowboy hat was cocked off to one side, and there was a red handkerchief around his neck. The look was completed with dirty chaps, boots, and spurs. He was pointing a revolver straight at me, barrel smoking. In the classroom I listened as my teacher, Mr. Johnson, talked about the history of the United States during World War II. When he spoke he breathed deep. It was as if talking and breathing were a physical exertion. He spoke of all the great men who had fought in various wars. He spoke of

Hitler and the Holocaust.

What were the women doing during World War II, I wondered. They were left out of history textbooks. Those books spoke about the men who had fought in our nation's wars and introduced us to the leaders in the country, none of whom were women. I really did not want to be hearing about this war from Mr. Johnson. I wished I were sitting next to my grammy, looking through her photo albums and hearing her tell me the stories instead.

I drifted off into a daydream.

I remembered thumbing through my grandparents' photo album, sitting next to my grammy. She was showing me pictures of my grandpa standing next to an airplane, his leather pilot hat down over his ears and strapped under his chin. On the outside of the plane were swastikas. I set my finger on the symbol that I'd come to know as a symbol of hate.

There was a number painted beside the swastikas. I asked my grammy what that was. "Those were the number of Nazi aircraft your grandfather shot down during World War II," she said proudly. Then she went on to tell me how evil Hitler was and the things that happened in those concentration camps. "How could anyone ever do that to other human beings?" she said, looking off into the distance with a look of deep sadness on her face. I wanted to change the subject, talk about something that was not so disturbing. So I asked her about her life on the Montana homestead, which shifted her mood, and we moved into much happier territory.

As my mind returned to the classroom after drifting off in thought, a gangly girl named Sarah raised her hand to ask a question. She had thick lenses in her glasses, which constantly fell down the bridge of her nose. She asked a question about the homework assignment. The teacher turned to some of the older boys in the class and they laughed and made fun of Sarah for not understanding her homework. I'd had enough. My heart racing and my underarms damp with sweat, I stood up. I told Mr. Johnson he should not treat students that way and that I was tired of the way he disrespected all of the students, especially the girls. His face turned red, like a tomato. Nearly spitting as he spoke, trying to hold back his anger, he told me to sit down. I did not sit down. He told me to go to the principal's office. I gathered up my books and my backpack and stormed out the door, glancing at the John Wayne poster as I left.

I wanted to walk right out of that class and never come back.

I slouched on a chair in the school office with my arms crossed. I told myself that I was going to get out of this jail. I looked around at the walls and the woman behind the desk. She had a permanent scowl on her face. I wondered if she was capable of smiling, or if the muscles in her face had formed from the constant frown and strain of her unhappiness. When I explained to my mother what had happened, she was furious at the teacher. She attempted to call a meeting with the teacher and the principal. The teacher never showed up, so instead of the principal confronting the situation, he switched me out of the class to another teacher.

After that incident, Sarah had thanked me with her eyes, peering over her glasses next to her locker, where she stood hunched over with her schoolbooks bundled in her arms. With that glance I knew I had shown her that she could stand up for herself. I wondered what would have become of her if I had not defended her that day in class. Possibly she would have taken the abuse not only from the teacher, but from a boyfriend or husband, never speaking up for herself again since that moment at age thirteen.

As school went on, I grew more and more disconnected, always longing to be somewhere other than where I was. I could not wait to get home and go outside to be with my horse in our front yard, surrounded by trees, listening to the rushing Snoqualmie River in the bottom of the valley.

I can still picture to this day the trees surrounding the little yellow house I grew up in. There was a huge King apple tree we harvested every year to make applesauce. Those apples were the size of a baby's head—perfectly plump and round. After my two sisters and I climbed up in the tree to pick the apples, we handed them down gently to Mom. We peeled and sliced them, simmering them in a big pot with some water until they got soft. With a hand masher, we pressed the apples firmly until they formed a chunky sauce. The applesauce simmered on the wood stove to thicken, and my mom added cinnamon and nutmeg until the entire house smelled of the sweet spice brewing within the apples.

I also loved the lilac trees that bloomed with beautiful purple and blue blossoms, the large Douglas fir trees, the cedar trees we used to climb, and the filbert trees that lined the road next to the horse barn. Those filberts were so delicious. On a good mast year the filbert nuts would weigh the branches of the trees down and cover the ground below in a blanket of light brown nuts.

The grey squirrels would enter frenetically through the filbert trees in the fall, collecting the nuts and hoarding them for later in the year when there were no nuts to be gathered. Sometimes I watched from a distance before I went up to the trees. The grey squirrels would jam a nut into their mouth and carry it to a spot on the ground, quickly bury it, and go back for another. I watched as the squirrels scattered their larder throughout the landscape. They buried nuts in all different locations around their territory. Standing in the shadow of the horse stall, I watched a squirrel, nut in cheek, glancing over his shoulder. He dug a hole, but did not bury the nut. He faked it, keeping the nut in his mouth, perhaps suspecting a jay or other intruder in the area that could have raided his winter cache. That squirrel must have had such a detailed map of spatial memory and of the scents specific to place. He could go back throughout the year to feed, especially during the cold winter when he needed to keep himself warm. I continued to watch as those grey squirrels chirped and flicked their tails at intruders, including the Steller's jay and me as I gathered filberts to roast over the fire on our woodstove.

This landscape was part of me. I was born in that house in the Snoqualmie Valley. The land, the waters, and all the living things there shaped how I perceived the world around me. I was a baby crawling on the soft grass, a child running barefoot on the damp leaves of the maple tree and picking those bittersweet grapes on the vines. Those times held some of my richest memories. I can even remember the distinct sound of the winter wren that sang on the very top of the cedar tree outside my bedroom window. This is the place that I would picture when I closed my eyes to fall asleep after I left home in search of the unknown.

On the way back from the hospital after my fall from Sundance, I stared out the window at the lush green forest blurring by. Everything looked different, the forest more alive than ever. The edges of the cedar trees' leaves glistened, their branching pattern mimicked the branches of the streams and rivers I had grown up around. I noticed a doe grazing in a field next to the road. A red-tailed hawk perched on top of a tree just before it swooped down in front of our truck. I was more aware of my surroundings than ever before. Every detail and disturbance jumped out at me like an explosion from a firecracker: crisp, clear, and full of wonder. Had those animals always been there and I was just noticing them for the first time? My new awareness felt somehow linked to the mysterious place I'd gone to after my fall.

Sitting in that old rusty Chevy pulling a horse trailer, I vowed that I would search for the unknown. I would discover why I was here on this earth and search for that light of comfort and peace through the long dark abyss. I felt trapped in my body, and my thoughts felt significant: I now knew so much more was possible beyond thought. I saw the world around me in a new light, where anything could happen.

It had taken nearly leaving this world to discover how much wonder it held.

Freedom

Though I couldn't see my whole path stretching before me, I knew for certain that I could not find what I was searching for by staying in school. Now that I had experienced something more—something untouchable yet definite—I knew I had to change my life. I wanted to see what was really going on in the world around me, to be free of the chains I felt when I sat at my desk in that concrete building that was, perhaps ironically, named after a Native American chief who raised his own children in a fishing village at the mouth of a nearby river with only longhouses for shelter. I sat motionless in that cold, hard chair, facing forward, listening to the dull tone of the teacher, under florescent lights, with tiny windows placed so high I could not see outside. I knew that was where I wanted to be: outside, free.

I looked for an escape, a way to break out from that institution where my future was molded to enter a generic workforce. I started to question the purpose of that workforce. After school I often went down to the river to explore the banks. I'd sit for hours, watching the river. How was I going to get out of here? I wanted to feel free, like the squirrel I watched gathering filberts every fall.

Outside of school, things were good. When we were all kids, growing up in our rural neighborhood, we had trails worn through the backyards of our neighbors: pathways of connectivity open for use by the local children. We sped from backyard to backyard on foot, bike, or horseback. There was a secret hideaway under the bridge down the road, where we kept a few broken chairs and a table. The older girls taught me about the birds and the bees, talked about boys, and made up jokes. We would all hop on our horses and ride down that small country road past the houses and down to the river. Every time there was a large stretch of lawn in front of a house, we would gallop our horses and then slide to a halt right before the driveway so the horses would not slip or damage their joints. Some of the neighbors would get upset because the hooves of the horses would make deep divots in their lawns. Those were the fun times, when we were all kids growing up together. Our only responsibility was to be home for dinner.

Things changed when my two sisters left home. The eldest, Serene, went off to college, and the other, Chantal, went traveling around the country with friends. I felt lonelier than ever. It was almost summer following the ninth grade. My mom had transferred me after eighth grade into a private school where the classes were small and the teachers actually looked the students in the eye. It was a big improvement from the concrete public school.

Just as my ninth-grade year was wrapping up for summer, I came home from the river one evening and saw a white VW bus in our driveway. Chantal was home for the first time after moving out months before. We had only heard from her a few times since she left. I was excited—now there was someone to talk to. She told me of her adventures, going to concerts, meeting people, being free from society.

"Most people just do what they're told, go to school, get a job, work for society, do what everyone else is doing. Nobody is really living the way they want to." I listened intently. I had questioned why people seemed so driven toward a career, focusing only on the outcome of becoming someone with a job, a house, a family, and nice things.

"On the road it's different," my sister said. "People have deep and meaningful conversations about life and the spirit world. You should come with us, Doniga."

My sister had brought a friend with her, Sprite. They stayed at our place for a few weeks, often just sitting out on the front porch talking for hours. I was very drawn to Sprite. She was short with freckles on her face and little dreadlocks sticking out every which way. When she talked to me, she looked me in the eye like she was looking into my soul. Her blue eyes sparkled with silver specks. She looked like what I'd imagined a fairy to look like, and I supposed that was how she got her name. She asked me about my life, what I liked to do, what I cared about. This was the first time one of my older sisters' friends had shown an interest in me. Sprite said they were headed back on the road to Oregon and asked if I wanted to go. Of course I said yes! This was what I had been waiting for: to escape my everyday life and get on the road, roaming free.

My father died at the hands of a drunk driver when I was still in the womb. My mother worked so hard to raise three girls by herself. She worked during the day in the Montessori preschool she had built in our backyard. Children would come every morning and my mother would teach them, using the philosophy of Maria Montessori. She taught them to use their senses, to work independently on activities of their choice. They made art, shared stories, and hiked in nature to study tadpoles and frogs. In the evenings she would go on night watch at the juvenile detention center in the next town in order to make ends meet. When she was not at work, she was in the garden, where we grew a lot of our own food, or chopping and stacking wood, fixing the horse fence, mowing the lawn, cleaning, or cooking. She provided for us, kept us fed with healthy food, gave us horses to ride, and brought us skiing every weekend in the winter. She filled the role of mother and father and she did all of this through her grief of losing her soulmate the night of his thirtieth birthday.

And yet, despite all she did for us, I acted without thought to her worry when Chantal and Sprite invited me along. My mom was at work when they were ready to hit the road. I sat on my bed upstairs and wrote her a note: *Mom, don't worry about me, I'll be all right. I'll be back before school starts. Love, Doniga.*

I was free, on the open road with no idea of where I was headed and no actual plan for returning home. A recklessness came over me, and I had not the slightest concern about leaving home at age fifteen.

After driving south through the night, Chantal, Sprite, and I found a spot to park the VW bus along a back road. It was dawn and we were next to a river. There were mountains all around. Chantal suggested we go swimming, so we stripped down naked and jumped in the river. I swam out into the middle, gasping for air. I remember feeling as if the core of my body would freeze as I lost all feeling in my extremities. The water rushed me downriver and I wasn't sure I would make it back to shore. I angled toward the bank, out of breath. It took everything in me, a rush of adrenaline, to get my arms to propel me through the water.

When I made it to the rocks on the shore and stepped out of the water, a surge came through me. A tingling warm feeling engulfed my entire body, like pricks of thorns all over my skin. Slowly I regained feeling in my fingers and toes and breathed the cool air into my lungs. I sat on the rocks on the bank, naked and exhilarated. An aliveness and happiness overtook my entire body. I laughed, thinking about the other kids back home and how they were probably stuck doing something boring—and here I was, sitting naked next to a mountain river. There was no one telling me how to be. Not my mother, not my schoolteachers. It was just me, free to be and do what I wanted. I ran around naked in that forest, laughing with sheer delight.

I quickly started to discover my own style. I wore patchwork pants and ratty shirts, and I stopped brushing my hair. I walked around with no fear of anything or anyone. We traveled for weeks in that white VW bus. We went from Portland to Cougar Hot Springs. We traveled from music festival to rainbow gatherings (loose-knit gatherings, held in forested areas, of people from across the globe focusing on peace and love). All across the west there were thousands of young people doing the same thing, going from one gathering to the next, living off the change in their pockets. The people around me weren't bothered by not having money; in fact, they looked down on anyone who did. I would hear things like, "Rich people are ruining our planet with all of their material distractions. All those fancy cars, TVs, and expensive clothes are killing the wild animals. All of their factories have paved over the forests, destroying thousands of species and suffocating the soil. At the same time society is at war with itself."

There was a contagious righteousness about the people I was hanging out with. I started to feel very angry at "those" people in society, the rich ones, the developers and the logging companies that were clear-cutting the forests. I grew up surrounded by timber companies and had observed their destructiveness as a little kid, riding by on my horse and seeing the forest cut down, the rain washing away the soil that the canopy had protected for thousands of years. But until now I had not translated my observations into anger and hatred. I was angry at the materialistic stuff created to make people look good or give people meaningless entertainment. I was mad that plastic was used and thrown away without a thought that those products would end up in the ocean, killing marine life. I and the people around me could live with what we had on our backs, making use of the waste society left behind. We did not need all the rich folks' trappings.

In the early mornings we'd find entire dumpsters full of bagels, bread, and produce. There was so much waste that none of us went hungry. We would sit on the streets of whatever town we were going through, someone with a guitar and others with drums, and sing songs and put out a change jar for tips. Some reached in their pockets and happily gave with a smile, but the majority of people either walked faster or steered clear, at times walking to the other side of the street to get around us.

Sleeping out under the stars with the universe surrounding me, I found a new way of living free. Since falling off Sundance the previous year, I had known there was more to life than going along with those around me. I wanted to carve a path toward meaning and connection, one of love and bliss. I felt like a meteor flying through the universe, on fire with the passion I found inside when I danced, sang, ran through the forest, spun fire on the ends of chains, and jumped in every river I came upon. I learned that summer to let go of self-doubt and express myself beyond the limitations of thought.

Calling

A nd yet, despite all that passion and my newfound, treasured freedom, despite my stubborn rebellion against convention, something deep inside was calling me back home.

The outward landscape of my homeland was mirrored inside me. Just as the orography of the Cascade mountain range encompassing my birthplace was formed by the rain, the wind, and the moving soils, I too was shaped internally by the elements, by what my senses had taken in since my birth. I longed for the distinct sound of the Snoqualmie River as my own internal waters awakened. The streams and rivers that surged through the Cascade Mountains across the land and boulders, over waterfalls and through the valleys, shaping each pathway in a dendritic (tree-like, branching) pattern, were like that of the blood inside my own heart, flowing out through my arteries.

And so I was torn. There was so much more to explore.

There were cultures to experience and adventures to be had. I had my newfound freedom, expressed by standing next to an interstate with my thumb in the air, or singing and dancing wildly under the full moon. But something continued to draw me back to where the cedar trees stood tall, covering the hills and mountains until they disappeared in an endless green sea of forest. They appeared in my dreams, dreams in which I was wild like the wolf and running with the elk.

I had made my way to Boulder, Colorado, with a group of reckless runaway teenagers. I had been on the road for a couple of months by then and had separated from Chantal and Sprite. There was a knot deep inside my stomach. My mother had been looking for me. She had gotten word to Chantal that she was incredibly worried and would do anything to get her baby back home safe. I wanted to call her and tell her I loved her, tell her I was safe and I missed her dearly and wanted to come home. I called from a payphone on the street of downtown Boulder and left a message, but I didn't say any of the things I wanted to say. Instead I told her I was on my path and I was not sure when I would be home. Why was I rebelling so much against her? I guess I needed something to rebel against, to justify my abandoning her.

In the park that lay above Boulder, a group of young people were talking about heading west. My ears perked up and I asked them where they were going. They said, "We're headed to the Hog Farm in California to see Wavy Gravy at the Pignic."

The Hog Farm was a place where activists who shared my views gathered in commune-style living. Wavy Gravy, who had the inspiration for the festival, was the official clown for the Grateful Dead and a legend amongst the hippie types. I had always wanted to see the Northern California coast, and it would get me closer to home.

I asked if I could hitch a ride. But suddenly, as we drove west down the interstate in an old Subaru, I lost my sense of freedom. I was trapped in a car with complete strangers. I felt caged once again. I stared out the window at the cars whizzing past, caught up in my thoughts, unaware of the conversation between the driver and other passengers. All of a sudden there was a jolt and the car started skidding off the road. I watched as the front driver-side wheel flew off into the next lane. I held onto the door in the back seat. My knuckles were white from me gripping the door handle as the car propelled forward on three wheels and one axle, screeching out of control. The driver managed to steer the car to a stop on the side of the interstate. I was far from home and I wanted so badly to keep going west. I wanted to make that car take me home.

With my heart racing and my entire body clammy, I grabbed my backpack and headed down the bank of the interstate. There was no time to discuss options. One of the runaways joined me. He and I walked silently down a side road until we got to the next on-ramp to the interstate. Backpack on and thumb in the air, I should have felt free, free to go and do whatever I wanted.

Truly, I was longing for the feeling of riding my horse through the woods. That was what I was looking for out on the highway, breeze in my hair, insecurities shedding off me like a horse sheds his winter coat. I no longer felt free out on the road as I had when I first left home. I only felt deeply afraid, insecure, and alone.

We caught a ride in an eighteen-wheeler, and I was asleep in the back seat of the sleeper when my hitchhiking partner shook me awake. "We need to get out of here." It was the middle of the night, but I jumped up as if awoken from a bad dream.

I grabbed my bag and leaped down the steps of the massive truck. The truck driver mumbled something I couldn't make out just as the passenger door closed. Once again we were on the side of the interstate in the dark, walking silently along the road. My hitchhiking partner had a disturbed look on his face. I wondered what had happened while I was asleep in that truck but didn't have the energy to open my mouth and say a word.

Exhausted, we followed the gravel shoulder until we arrived at a bridge. I walked down the steep embankment and heard the river. I felt a wave of home wash over me. Memories rushed in of all those years growing up, swimming and playing in the river, riding my horse down to the boat launch in my bathing suit and swimming across the river with my horse by my side. The sound of the river was always in the background when I stepped out my front door. That steady sound was the one thing I could count on when my emotions were like water raging out of control.

I pulled out my sleeping bag and just wanted to crawl in and disappear from the world. My hitchhiking partner was still silent and set up his bed close to mine. Finally, as I felt the river rocks beneath me, I started to let my guard down. That was when he reached over and grabbed me. He started to kiss me. I was avoiding it. The rest happened like a blur: I yelled stop. He kept going. I pushed him away. He pulled in closer. He entered into me. I cried. I wanted it to stop. It was a tornado that I was desperate to escape from. When the tornado stopped I ran to the bank of the river. He went to his sleeping bag and I sat weeping. I never imagined my first time would be like this.

I had been longing for solace in the wilderness. I wanted to be away from the cruel human world. As I traveled the country, I did not find what I was searching for. Instead I found desecration of what was most precious to me. I saw large tracts of land destroyed by development, smokestacks punctuating skylines, and crop dusters spraying chemicals on growing food. And I had also become disillusioned with the lifestyle of the road and the people I was interacting with. The young people around me were living out of their cars or on the streets, traveling from festival to festival. They seemed to be searching for something that I was not; possibly they were just looking for the next high. They were waiting for a small white square of paper on their tongue that sent them away from the earth, to get them to a place that I am not sure actually exists outside of the high. Possibly they were searching for connection in a fragmented society. The revolution of the sixties and seventies—my parents' time to shine—brought the "back to the land" movement. Many of those from my parents' generation were fueled by drugs, and their vision of connecting with the land was never fully realized. The drug became what they craved above all else; it placated them enough that they never pursued the purity of true connection with nature. I realized that the same seemed to be true of the kids I was with on the road that summer.

After being raped I parted ways with the hitchhiker who assaulted me. I couldn't bring myself yet to admit I'd given up on my freewheeling summer, and rather than feeling defeated and going home, despite my longing for it, I hitchhiked by myself to the Hog Farm. I arrived in a daze and looked out at the sea of colorful people looking so joyous and free, though with my new disillusionment, I wondered if this was just a chemically induced figment. I wandered around the crowds of hippies sitting in circles, playing music, laughing, juggling, and dancing. I attempted to join in the festivities as I listened to the music that was thundering from the main stage out into the parking lot. There were girls my age sitting on the backs of tailgates, spinning in circles, dancing in long patchwork dresses. They looked so pretty. I thought I should be dancing, looking pretty, but I felt very ugly. I hid my face with my fat dreadlocks that I had shaped after leaving home two months before, not brushing or washing my hair. I wore baggy clothes to hide my body.

I saw a familiar face by a VW bus, and I approached. Clover, a full-figured girl about twenty-one years old, stood there slumped up against the van. I had last seen her at the rainbow gathering in Oregon. When I reached her, she gave me a warm hug, then we began to talk about our travels. I told her that I had just hitched from Colorado and she reminisced about her travels there and the beautiful mountains and rivers. She told me she and some friends were headed out to the coast and then driving north. I asked if I could get a ride.

As we rounded the bend of Fish Hatchery Road, following the curves in the river, I finally felt deep relief. Home. We drove up the driveway to the little yellow house where I was born. My mother stood outside with a gaggle of preschool children awaiting their parents. Heavy backpack on my back, I strode confidently up to her. Tears rolled down her face as she embraced her baby girl, back at last. Although my mother and oldest sister, Serene, had spent the summer trying to find me, acting upon their heartache and my betrayal of them, none of it mattered in that moment. I was home.

As a teenager in the 1990s I started to become aware of a change in my neighborhood. Within one generation, from the 1980s to the 1990s, alteration of behavior in the children resulted in an adaptation of the landscape. I returned home after the summer away, and I noticed the kids' trails were beginning to disappear. Instead, large fences were being built around yards. The fences were solid wood and so high you could not even see over the top. In the years to follow, horses left the yards and were replaced by fancy cars and boats. All the trails we took as kids to get down to the river became overgrown with blackberry bushes.

What had happened to all the kids? Where were they? When I was young, there had been no high-tech workers in our rural town. People we knew were teachers, plumbers, farmers. That was until the mid-1990s, when the nearby Microsoft office started to expand and the people who worked there needed to find places to live. I started to see a shift in the way kids looked. They were spending less time outside and more time hunched over a computer or video game. Rosy cheeks were replaced by pale skin—a sign of too much time spent indoors. The kid trails started to disappear. Sticks and pinecones were replaced with handheld video games. Years later, I'd come to find out after reading a book entitled *Last Child in the Woods* that what I noticed in my neighborhood was happening across the country: from 1997 to 2003, half of the children that used to cut across backyards and make fishing poles to cast in the river no longer spent time outside (Hofferth and Sandberg 2001).

In 1996, the year I left for the summer, something shifted in the kids in the Fall City neighborhood—they no longer had a reason to go outside. With everything readily available at their fingertips and the average household income rising, there was no desire or need to plant a garden, raise chickens, or milk a cow. The children suffered what the author of *Last Child in the Woods,* Richard Louv, calls Nature-Deficit Disorder.

As I struggled to reintegrate, I found myself still longing for something out of reach. I hadn't found it in the private school my mother sent me to, and I hadn't found it out on the road or at the rainbow gatherings. The closest I'd ever come was in my idyllic childhood, camping and backpacking with my family. My mom, sisters, and I used to find a spot by a river or the Puget Sound and set up a tent, cook over a fire, and enjoy throwing rocks in the water and catching crabs or crawdads. It was in the wild where I felt at home. Now, after my summer of supposed freedom on the road, I found the call of the wild stronger than ever.

This kind of calling was once something that did not need to be found. It wasn't even a call; it was a way of life, it was home. It was there when a young child would learn the basics of life and survival: shelter, fire, water, and food. Children who were born into a traditional Indigenous tribe or clan would have known the plants, animals, birds, and all life that surrounded them, because it was their home and their survival depended on it. They may have grown up strapped to their mother's back as she went out to gather plants or dig roots. They would have learned the dangers of the wild as they began toddling around so as not to cross a poisonous snake or stumble upon a predator. They would have also learned to track to find out who was stalking their tribe when darkness and sleep took over.

I yearned to find that deep connection to the earth. Going for hikes and walking on top of the land was not allowing me to truly experience it. I needed immersion, training, and a community of people that would keep me motivated. I no longer believed endless resources for limitless extraction existed. I was questioning everything: the food I ate, the house I lived in, and the clothes I wore. I knew that the apples I picked from our front yard came directly from the earth. The vegetables we grew and the chicken eggs from the coop all came directly from the land and soil. But where did everything else come from? I had never thought to ask that question before. Where was the food that I picked up at the grocery store grown? What about the cotton that was woven into my clothes—how many stops did it make before it was lying against my skin? I started to see I was disconnected—disconnected in such a way that I was harming the life that I loved, the only thing at that time that felt authentic and important.

Again I wanted to run, but this time into the wild. I was not ready to fall back into the life of the average teenager. I felt a real urgency to make a change.

Home from the road two weeks, I was in our front yard taking care of our horses when a friend of my mother's drove up. Patricia was a healer, with beautiful long black hair with contrasting silver streaks hanging below her shoulders and a smile that seemed to stretch across most of her face, with big white teeth. I quickly finished brushing my horse when she drove up. I felt a kinship to her because she had helped me heal from the trauma of my head injury after falling from Sundance.

In the passenger seat sat a man I had never seen before. His dark, weathered face was round and he had a look of deep wisdom. As he opened the door he hoisted himself out of the car with a worn wooden cane topped with a large jade stone. He had a presence about him I had not experienced in any other human. It was as if his spirit was much larger than his body. I would come to find out later there was great significance in this meeting. Patricia introduced him as Macki Ruka. He was an elder medicine man from the Waitaha Maoris, a matriarchal culture in New Zealand (Inglish 2017). He learned from the grandmothers of his tribe the sacred celestial ways of his people, the ceremonies and the prophecies. When he was only seven years old, he was instructed to swim with the dolphins and the whales to learn directly from the wild creatures of the sea and how they navigated (Crystal 1997). This type of Indigenous upbringing was what I had been searching for. If I had grown up in an intact culture such as Macki's, I would have been guided along my search—and what I thought of now as a search would simply have been the way of my people.

He surveyed our front yard as if looking for an enemy hiding in the brush. His gaze stopped when he saw me standing there with a grain bucket in one hand and a currycomb in the other. He locked eyes with me like he was piercing my armor. Then his face softened into a smile. Another man, Josh, stepped out of the back seat of the car. Josh had long hair pulled back in a ponytail and wore earth-tone clothing. He walked as if he was about to step on hot coals, kind of floating.

I brought the group over to meet the horses. The elder looked at me as I petted Sundance. He said to me, "You are headed for danger if you continue on the path you are on." I had not said anything but hello, and here he was telling me what I needed to do with my life. My first reaction was to rebel, say I was on a fine path living my own life, but there was something about the way he spoke, the look in his eye, and the feeling I got around my heart. I knew he was right.

He went on to say, "You need to study at a school called the Wilderness Awareness School. At this school you will learn about Mother Nature setting the frequency of all life. You will use nature to heal the hurts within yourself. Here you will learn that the longest journey you will take is from your mind to your heart, and then even longer is the journey from your heart back to your mind. It is only when you find unity with yourself and the universe that you will find unconditional love in all that you do."

Macki did not say much else that afternoon as my mother made lunch and we all ate together. He sat observing while the group chattered away, catching up on life. That afternoon, through a chance meeting, my lifelong journey into learning the language of nature was authenticated. I felt I had direction and purpose, like a migrating bird who knows that heading in one direction will bring brighter days and abundant nourishment.

Awareness

Wilderness Awareness School, or WAS, as we called it, was designed for kids who did not fit in with the average teenager; it was for outcasts of the contemporary school system. By that point I certainly fit that description. I had retained my style from the road: my new fat dreadlocks on my head, secondhand clothing, and hair on my legs. My classmates at this new school ranged from high-school dropouts to highly motivated unschoolers that had an intense drive to learn every plant, animal, and tracking and survival skill, pushing themselves to their limits in extreme conditions within the elements of nature. We formed the first cohort of a maverick pack of teenagers, each as individual and strong-willed as the next, but brought together by one common thread: nature.

The curriculum was a grand experiment to take kids raised with modern amenities and immerse them in the wilderness, mentor them by asking a lot of questions to invoke passions, and teach them self-awareness and leadership. At WAS, students learned to survive in the wilderness, how to extract medicine and food from wild plants, how to track animals, and how to understand the language of nature. We were allowed to be free from authority and commands, the reason most of us stayed for years. We worked things out as they came up.

Most days, we wandered in the forest with no destination or agenda. When we arrived at a spot that felt right in the forest, we gathered wood. Even on the wettest days—most days in Western Washington—we all knew where to find the fine, dry twigs hanging dead under the boughs of a hemlock, cedar, or fir tree. We peeled the soft bark of the red cedar and broke it apart to form a nest, just like the squirrels did to line their nests. We worked together to spin a hand drill on a flat board to form a coal, and then we moved the coal into our nest, which would go up in flames as we softly blew on the ember.

Once the fire was lit, we sat around it and talked, which seemed like the most natural thing to do. The group of us—Justin, Rikki, Terry, Michael, Essa, Greg, and I—gathered and talked about what we wanted to do, what excited us. The fire was our unifying force and has continued to warm our friendships throughout the full circle of our lives together.

We had our routines. We each had a spot that we called our secret spot, where we went to sit and observe. We had our favorite tracking areas, where the predators frequented watering holes. Climbing trees, taking a nap on top of moss as soft as goose down, and jumping into lakes were all common activities for a day at school.

On one occasion, a few months after I started at the school, I became very perturbed by one of my classmates, Michael. He had brown hair down to his shoulders that he pulled back into a low ponytail. He wore loose-fitting clothes and small stubbles of hair were just starting to emerge for the first time from his face. I could never figure out his voice—was it going to come out high or low? He started stepping on my heels that day, tripping me, walking into my personal space and generally being annoying.

There was a bank to the side of the old logging road we were walking on. I let him get close, and without notice, I pushed him down the hill. When he stood at the base of the hill, his clothes covered in moist dirt and decomposing maple leaves, he had no words, but looked at me with respect, like a wolf that's just established a boundary with another member of the pack. From then on Michael and I were good friends, and he was clear on the boundaries of our friendship.

We learned to immerse ourselves in our senses and the natural world by delving deep into connecting with nature and ourselves. The only thing we were instructed to do was to follow our passion—and each of my classmates had one. Michael, for example, eventually grew out of his awkward teenage years and became a master bow maker and archer. He went on to become a luthier, making beautiful instruments prized by musicians. His cellos and violins are used at venues like Carnegie Hall. We all found and engaged with our passions by directly communicating with the natural elements of the Pacific Northwest forests we immersed ourselves in.

There were a couple of adults with us, Anne and Chris, but they never paid much attention and were typically out of sight or observing quietly. Anne was sweet, like a favorite aunt, with a warm smile and a gentle voice. Chris was usually working on his own skills of survival or tracking, often being goofy and cracking jokes, hoping that we would just see him as one of us. Once in a while they would ask us questions. But in general, the seven of us were free to do anything. We were hanging out along a river, exploring ponds, and finding new mysteries in the forest each day.

Early on, we learned how to weave baskets, and the thrill of creating something from natural materials immediately engaged me. I spent much of my time weaving by the river. It helped me calm my inner turmoil when I still had a great deal of it. It helped me to focus my hands on a task and my intentions into the future, let me release the past and put my brain in the present moment when I still struggled to do so. I would sit and weave the pliable willow, smelling the earthy, pungent scent of the bark. I held the wefts in my fingers, those branches that I wove over and under, as I cradled the basket between my legs and shaped the warps, the branches that supported the structure. Once the basket was finished I put straps on it so I could carry it on my back. The baskets I wove were useful both to my mind and to our other pursuits; I'd often fill them with the food I was learning to forage to take back to our simple huts to cook over a fire.

We called one place in the forest the Nasties. To be clear, the environment there was anything but nasty. There were large western red cedar trees with moss-covered logs lying at their bases. We nibbled at the leaves of wild ginger where it grew in patches of light that filtered through the canopy overhead like strings of golden thread. We called that place the Nasties because it was a party spot, and often we found trash that was just plain nasty left by the previous weekenders. We cleaned it up, sometimes filling our handwoven baskets with the disgusting garbage left by revelers in a jarring juxtaposition, and hoped the place would be treated better by the next weekend's revelers.

We loved to hike out to a place we called Osprey Swamp. There was an osprey nest at the top of one of the dead standing alders, and often when we arrived we caught a glimpse of the bird fishing in the waters below. We would walk out to the middle of the swamp by balancing on the logs floating throughout. Then began the game of trying to make each other fall into the water below. We ran from log to log, sparring with each other, waiting for the first to go down. Most would eventually fall in, then trudge out of the water dripping wet while bellows of laughter erupted from everyone else.

We would play epic games of capture the flag in the middle of the wet forest. During the game we would jump over logs, belly crawl, and sneak through the wet leaves of the understory. I can still recall the smell of the decomposing duff. As my face touched the forest floor I would notice all the white hyphae of fungi as it spread from one spot on a leaf and formed white finger-like filaments to eventually consume the leaf entirely. The slime mold, the grubs, the spiders, and the earthworms were all working to make food from the waste of the forest. The smell of the rot was sweet, not stagnant, as the leaves and debris worked their way down the layers, forming into humus and eventually ending up as dirt to feed the cycle of growth. The moisture on the forest floor allowed the plants and animals to each perform their role in decomposition.

I made new discoveries like the generative decay of the forest floor every single day, and I made them through direct observation. I was engaging my senses in such a complete way that those discoveries would embed into my very being. This was so much closer to the feeling of freedom I'd been seeking, because it wasn't a selfish, I-do-what-I-want freedom, the freedom that had felt so hollow after my months on the road. This was the freedom of knowing that all life is interconnected, and that my choices and actions affected the beautiful wild world around me, the freedom that came with knowing I was a wild creature connected with all other wild creatures. I was learning firsthand about ecology, not as an external human observer but as a strand in the web of life. This was school—or more accurately, unschool. What a distance I had come from my days in the concrete box.

Still, it took me a long time to learn to shake off the constructs of our culture and uncover my own wildness, to be able to blend into the forest so I could truly see what was around me in its natural state. Learning to track was essential to this development. When I first started at WAS I had never really discovered tracks or tracking. I might have seen some marks in the ground or animals in the distance, and I knew what to do if I got in a dangerous situation with a bear or a mountain lion. What I did not know was how to detect if the animals were around by the signs they left behind.

One of my classmates, Greg, was really into tracking. He always wore beige shorts and an earth-tone brown shirt and he mostly went barefoot, even if it was cold or wet. As he walked he rolled his feet down on the ground so carefully that he barely made a sound. He was quiet and either had a serious look on his face or a sideways smile. He was always drawing plants or trees or animal tracks in his journal. I had never known anyone who drew or even followed tracks. I didn't initially see what the big deal was.

One day I followed Greg upriver, along the bank paralleling the Snoqualmie. He kept pausing to look at tracks. I paused too, looked around, and threw rocks into the river. I got impatient with how slowly he was traveling up the river, and I went on ahead. I saw some marks in the sand and decided to take a closer look. Greg was so interested in even the smallest pinprick of a mark; I wanted to know what he found so fascinating. Each of the marks I found had five toes and an indent under the toes that was curved in a C shape. The toes were connected with a line, like they were attached toward the tip of the toe. There were sharp points at the tip of each toe, like someone had stuck a pin in the sand.

The riverbank dropped off into a steep bank and I could see drag marks in the ground that looked as though something had slid down and landed in the river below. I kept following the marks. They would disappear into the river and reappear further down. It looked as though whatever animal had left tracks had been using the bank like a waterslide into the water, then coming out and doing it again.

Greg sidled up with that funny walk he had. He approached the marks, kneeled down, looked close, and scratched his chin. I pretended I was not that interested, but really I was exuberant inside, so excited that I had possibly found tracks Greg was interested in. He started asking me questions.

"Where did the animal come from?"

I cocked my head to look at him. He was the tracker—why was he asking me?

When I did not answer, he continued to ask questions. "Where did it go? What was it doing? How was it moving? Why was it coming out of the water?"

I got frustrated with him.

"It came out of the river, went up the hill, and slid down the bank," I said.

He rubbed his chin and said, "Hmmm." After a pause, he asked, "What kind of animals that live around here spend time in the water?"

"Beaver, muskrat…" I trailed off. Suddenly I remembered sitting by the bank of the river when I was a little girl, seeing an animal come out of the water. "River otter!" I said.

He looked at me and said, "Hmm, river otter?"

I was not sure if I was right, and frustratingly, Greg wouldn't tell me. But I had to admit, my interest in tracking, which had previously seemed a bit dull to me, was piqued.

The curriculum at WAS, like everything there, was optional; our activities had to come from our own desire to learn and engage. The curriculum was developed by the founder of the school, Jon Young, and was called the Kamana Naturalist Training Program (Young 1996).

The program was an independent study that included journaling every species of mammal, bird, tree, and plant within my bioregion, followed by studying how it was all interconnected and the big picture of the ecology of the area. It was very different from how I had learned the sciences in school, where everything was separated into its own subject and not seen as part of the whole. I was given exercises to do on a daily basis to train my brain to the natural patterns I was immersing myself in, exercises like meticulously recording the weather four times during the day, along with other observations about the birds, trees, animals, and plants. We learned how to give thanks by naming each group of life forms on the earth and out into the sky. This was called the Thanksgiving Address. Chief Jake Swamp, sub-chief of the Wolf Clan of the Mohawk Nation, visited us during our time at WAS, and he wrote that section of the study guide. He believed that if every child learned to say thank you to all of creation when the sun rises each day, then there would be peace on earth. When I ran away from home I had longed to live close to the earth, but I did not know how to achieve that. Now I was training in methods that would bring me toward a deep nature connection like that of hunter-gatherer children who depended on those skills for survival.

After receiving the curriculum binder, which seemed to weigh as much as a baby, I sat down and opened the first book of Kamana. I sat in my bedroom and read through the exercise of finding a secret spot. It had to be a place close to home that I could visit every day. Right away a spot came to my mind. I had fond memories of going down to my neighbor Mark's pond when I was growing up, of watching the Great Blue Herons voling in the nearby field. The heron walked quietly in the meadow, lifting its legs high, stalking silently. It would find a place in the meadow and stop before it stabbed at a vole, catching the small rodent between its beak. The heron's long neck would bulge as the vole made its way down. I touched my hand to my own throat, imagining what it would feel like to have a rodent nearly the size of a rat work its way into my belly.

I had stopped going to Mark's pond many years before. I was busy with horse shows and pony club. I remembered now all the time I had spent catching frogs there, scaring my sisters by setting one on their shoulder, and sitting on the pond's bank with a fishing pole in hand. As I continued to read through the exercise, I knew this was an opportunity to connect with the pond again and relive my childhood memories.

I was instructed to go and sit and journal my observations. My journals included the weather and the birds, tracks, plants, and trees around me. Journaling was a way to demark the changes in the season and the rhythms of the life I was experiencing.

The first time I walked down to the pond to begin my exercise, three raccoons looked up at me curiously. One of the smaller ones walked closer for a better view while the other two kept pushing on toward the grove of cottonwood trees. I took that as a good sign. I found a place to sit. That lasted about five minutes before I got bored and started walking around, climbing trees, trying to occupy my restless mind.

As time went on, I found myself going to my secret spot more and more. Each time, I sat longer. When I was away, my thoughts wandered to the pond. I wondered what the animals were doing throughout their day as I went about mine. After my initial experience with the curious raccoons, I assumed I'd be able to watch all the animals that lived there going about their daily activities. I pictured the coyote lying in its daybed, licking itself, and the deer calmly grazing in the meadow, unperturbed by my presence. But it wasn't working that way. Every once in a while I would see deer run in the distance. I tracked the deer and the coyote, but no matter what time of day I came down, I just couldn't catch sight of the animals up close.

At WAS they would tell us stories of trackers so skilled they could get close enough to the animals to reach out and touch them. That level of ability, to connect that way with the wild creatures, was inspiring, and I found passion growing inside me to become a tracker.

I practiced my awareness and journaled my observations in minute detail, writing it all down and drawing maps. The topography of the landscape started to emerge from those maps. I would draw a new map each day with an X in the middle where I sat. I put landmarks in each of the four directions and would note observations correlated with their location. If a bird called or sang while I was there, I wrote that down. If a flower came into bloom, I drew it out. The hawks flying overhead, the deer bounding away, the first buds of spring, and the raccoon tracks along the bank all made their way onto my map. I added the grove of cottonwood trees to the southwest of where I sat, and then the red-winged blackbirds that I heard calling beyond the trees with their *chi-cho-reeee* song. When I returned home I would pore over field guides, studying the natural history and identification of all the life I was discovering around me.

One day, I walked over to the grove of cottonwood trees, wondering why there was always so much bird life coming from that direction. I climbed up a dirt bank, looked down, and discovered another pond in the middle of the grove of trees, secluded from the rest of the valley. There was a stream leading into the pond that seemed much too small to fill the body of water. There were piles of sticks from the wood of red alder, willow, and cottonwood trees forming a dam at the downstream side. Near the edge there was a large mound of sticks and logs. The discovery made my heart race. I had been merely four hundred yards away from this place for months with no idea.

On the edge of the pond there were stumps. It looked like a hatchet had felled the tree from all sides, the bits of wood falling to the ground below to form a carpet of woodchips. Next to the stumps was a channel leading out into the open water. It was a masterfully engineered paradise with birds singing, frogs jumping, damselflies swooping along the surface, and lush plants and trees of all kinds thriving. There were no signs of human trails leading in as I worked my way through the thicket of blackberries that surrounded the area like a thorny barricade.

I found a spot carpeted with soft mosses and grass. With my back against a cottonwood tree, I sat and marveled. That smell of the cottonwood buds came over me, reminding me of my childhood play spot at recess time, and I smiled joyfully. I felt like naturalist John Muir discovering the Yosemite Valley for the first time, reveling in the sheer beauty of this new place. After some time I saw a brown animal swimming in the water. With my back against the furrowed bark of the cottonwood, I practiced the sense meditation I'd been learning in order to blend in with my new secret place.

I listened with deer ears, imagining that my ears were large like those of the mule deer, whose name came from the sheer size of their ears. I listened for the quietest sound off in the distance, the far-off river flowing and the sweet quiet chirp of a dark-eyed junco. I smelled with a coyote nose. I pictured in my mind the long nose of the coyote that extends out in front of the face, leading the way through the hunt or alerting of a scent that could bring danger. I breathed deep, in through my nose, inhaling the scents in the air. Some were subtle, like the smell of the pond water; others, like the cottonwood buds, permeated my olfactory system. I tasted with a cat's tongue, imagining my taste buds were enlarged like a cat's. I felt with a raccoon's touch, using my body to feel my surroundings, like a raccoon as she navigates the bank of the pond with incredibly sensitive fingers. I watched with owl eyes, not moving my gaze but instead expanding my peripheral vision until the sides of my vision blurred.

All of these senses working together kept my mind from distraction and kept me from getting so excited that the animal coming toward me would notice me. As the animal swam closer, I continued to blend with my surroundings. I pictured the cottonwood tree I was leaning on wrapping its bark around me until I disappeared into its embrace. The creature crawled up the pond bank. I stayed stone still, continuing to view this animal only with my peripheral vision, never straight on. At that point it was four feet from me, along the bank to my left. It came closer and then froze. I could not help but shift my gaze to get a better look at the slick, wet, lustrous animal.

I looked into the small black beady eyes toward the top of its head. In between its eyes, protruding out, was a shiny black nose. Small ears protruded out slightly on the sides of the head.

This animal had built its place. It was the master designer of this ecotopia. The beaver now standing on webbed feet before me was shaping this land in a way that not only sustained the life of its own family, but also supported the rejuvenation of so many other forms of life. I could not contain the thrill of having a wild animal go about its daily life and swim up to me as if I were not there.

Then, in an instant, the beaver scented me. It spun around, took two bounds, and dove into the water. With its giant tail it whacked the surface of the pond. I jumped up at the sound. After it made its warning smack, it dove down and disappeared from sight.

I'd spent months going to my secret spot and had only observed animals from a distance. Now euphoria came over me and I collapsed on the ground, my cheek to the moist soil. I had experienced an unfathomable explosion of my senses. As I lay there on the ground and felt the earth wrapping her arms around me, I was flooded with gratitude. This moment had shown me that my life was going in the right direction. I felt energized, rejuvenated by the life-force of the earth.

But I had more to achieve. I resolved that I would see every single animal that lived in the area surrounding my secret spot, not just from a distance but so close that I could reach out and touch them.

After the beaver, all the wildlife in my secret spot started to accept me, one by one. I figured out where all the birds fed, nested, and roosted. As I approached each bird's territory, I would walk far enough away so as not to alarm them. I always knew that I had succeeded when I got to the secluded pond and the beaver was still swimming around or the American robin did not pause in his song as I walked under the branch he was singing on.

But there was a group of deer living in the meadow that I still hadn't been able to get close to. Usually my presence set off their natural trepidation and they would flee. Maybe they could predict which way I would come from, and when (typically right at dawn or dusk). Those deer started to permeate my thoughts throughout the day and as I would go to sleep at night.

I realized I had to find new ways to get to my secret sit spot. If I always headed off the road, down the driveway, to the edge of the meadow, and over to my cottonwood tree, surely the deer could anticipate my arrival. Could they possibly be ducking into the shadows to await my departure, at which time they would all go back to feeding? Every time I went to my secret spot I found deer tracks. I followed the tracks the deer had left when they walked slowly through the meadow on their trail.

I began to form a picture in my mind of the patterns of the deer, as if I was watching them from above. When I was off from WAS for a weekend, I headed to the meadow to take a look around. Doe tracks in the soft silt drew me in to follow them. I pictured the doe walking slowly, lifting her feet up high over the grasses and brush. She had placed her hind feet directly into the tracks of the front, leaving two tracks, joining together as if they were one, in the shape of an elongated heart. I was gaining enough tracking skill now to be able to imagine her motions from the tracks and signs she'd left.

I glanced to the side of the deer trail to see where she had browsed the willow and maple saplings. She left rough cuts when she pulled on the plants, her bottom incisors pushed up against the rough hard palate of skin and bone on the top jaw, where she lacked teeth in the front. Slowly chewing, she'd stopped and reached up for the new shoots of the willow. She pulled the branches away, ripping them, resulting in a straight but rough break. As she came across a young hemlock tree, she used those lower incisors to scrape the bark, eating the sweet cambium layer. I pictured her stopping there, head motionless, absorbing the landscape around her with her soft eyes. Her tracks showed me each time she had turned her head. There was a slight pressure to the side of the track where she turned her head and the front track was angled towards the direction she looked. She paused roughly every ten paces or whenever she heard a sound or caught a scent on the breeze. She used a worn trail that branched out into less-used trails, where she could find forage on the diverse plants. There were signs of deer everywhere at my secret spot, tracks that showed them calmly walking and feeding, an indication that they were not stressed.

I decided to start taking a different path to my secret spot each time—I thought I would trick the deer by not being predictable. I jogged down the road in the opposite direction of Mark's pond, along the bank of the river early one morning, before the sun. As I paused at the river, I saw something off in the distance. I was thinking that it looked like a beaver crossing over the bank of the river. I looked closer. Off in the distance, the creature came up on the bank. I did not see a huge beaver tail dragging behind it. The light was still dim in the dawn, but I started to make out the animal's features. It had a sleek tail and resembled a dog but low to the ground. It had a long pointed snout and looked like it had a destination and would attack anything that got in its way. A river otter. I sat there quietly, willing myself not to make any noise. Another river otter came out of the water. I watched them up on the bank as they started playing. They wrestled and then slid down the bank and into the water.

I had figured it out! It *had* been a river otter sliding down the bank. That was the track I'd seen on the riverbank months ago with Greg! I imagined them swimming under the water, bubbles rising up on their silvery and brown sleek fur. Once they went underwater where I could not see them, I imagined those otters swimming, catching fish, and loving life so much they had to celebrate by coming out of the water to play and slide down the muddy riverbank.

That was my first tracking experience where I saw the mystery tracks first and kept a question in my mind, not knowing who had left the tracks, but hoping I would someday find out.

It had taken me months to figure out the answer, but the process was so much more valuable than if Greg had just told me.

I continued toward my secret spot, immensely aware that the journey was just as, if not more, rewarding than the destination. When I approached the neighboring golf course on the south side of my secret spot, I ran across the green so I wouldn't get caught trespassing. I was breathless when I reached the outer edge of the pond, and I slowly approached my spot, which was still far across the large meadow, over a football field away from the place where the deer would graze. Often I would see the group of deer when I came from below the meadow through the thicket of trees. Every time I got a little closer. It was typically a group of four does who would place themselves strategically in the grazing area like spokes on a wheel, facing out in the four directions.

I had come to the point with my daily visits where I could be on the edge of the meadow in the shadows, watching the deer in their relaxed habits, and they would behave as if no intruder or predator was present. But that day, after my victorious identification of the otters, I moved into the open and they quickly pronked away, all four feet leaving the ground and landing at once, putting a long distance between us before they slowed to a trot and glanced back to see that I wasn't chasing them. This had been happening every time I tried to get close. I wanted to exchange breath with the deer. I thought that maybe I needed to live with them if I wanted them to accept and not fear me.

So I brought my sleeping bag and slept out under the stars next to the meadow every day for a week. Maybe if I lived there, went about my daily business, the deer would get used to me. But I couldn't really start squatting on my neighbor's property full-time. Then I thought, what if I left something of mine there all the time? I brought down a smelly old shirt that I would often wear. It was a flannel button-up. I rubbed it on my underarms to make sure I got a good scent on it. (At that time in my life, I was not bathing often outside of jumping into a cold river or lake.) I left the shirt hanging from the willow grove above the place where the deer bedded. I put it where it was very visible; the deer would stumble across it frequently. I continued to go to the edge of the meadow, with each visit getting a bit closer to the deer.

Fox walking and owl eyes were the two things I practiced when I was approaching the deer. One of my mentors at WAS had taught me those were the two most important things to practice in nature. It was like a walking meditation. The red fox has fine hairs growing in between the toes and heel pad of its feet, helping to buffer the sound of the footstep. These hairs are visible when the track is in fine substrate like moist silt. The red fox also moves with a steady gate, head on a level plane, not bouncing up and down, allowing it to see subtle movements of mice as they scurry on the side of the trail. I set my feet down softly, the ball of my foot reaching forward to touch the earth, then slowly the rest of my foot comes down. Then, pulling my weight forward onto the ball as if I were feeling in the dark barefoot to avoid sharp protruding objects, I move silently.

Owls can see with their peripheral vision without moving their eyes around—their eyes are fixed in their skull and can't move. The owl's eye is so large that it accounts for 1 to 5 percent of its body weight, depending on the species (Lewis 2015). So I practiced reaching my vision out as far as I could while keeping my eyes still in their sockets, the way I had the day the beaver approached me. I made sure I could see what was to the left and right of me as well as what was on the ground and in the sky while keeping my eyes straight. I could not focus on any one thing in owl eyes and my vision got slightly blurred, but every movement jumped out at me like someone waving a flag.

Much of what I learned at WAS was an unlearning of what I had learned in public school. In public school we were taught to focus on the teacher, the textbook, or the computer screen. Movement and awareness were never a study, or even mentioned by a teacher except in the negative ("Stop moving around; eyes off your neighbor's page!"). Now I was practicing fox walking and owl eyes everywhere I went. As I moved and paused along the deer trail, I went into a sense meditation until I got to the point where I could get so deep into my senses that all thought drifted away into an undifferentiated nothingness. In those instantaneous moments, when I had no judgment of the past or future, my body became buoyant. Edges started to soften as the air and earth no longer felt separate from my physical body.

About six months into my daily routine of traveling to my sit spot, studying the deer and hoping they would accept me, I woke up before my alarm went off. It was still dark. Not only did I leave a shirt behind at my secret spot, but I felt like part of me was always there, even dreaming of my secret spot and the deer. I told myself this was the morning that something spectacular would happen at my secret spot. It was a cold morning, and I put my clothes on and rubbed my eyes open. I loved those early mornings when I awoke in the darkness and witnessed the transformation from dark to light. It's the time when the silence of night is only broken by the call of the great horned owl or the song of the tree frog. As the light started to emerge along the horizon, the robins awoke and soon the song sparrows and towhees erupted. Within a short period of time, the cacophony overwhelmed me as distinctions became less apparent and the edges of sound softened into one another.

The lights were still out in the houses I walked by on the neighborhood street. I had the beauty of birdsong on a spring morning and the dew on the blades of grass all to myself. I felt sorry for everyone asleep in their beds with their shades drawn. They had no idea what they were missing. Ahead, I saw a raccoon rambling across the road and into a culvert. Maybe it was the same raccoon that had greeted me curiously six months before, all grown up and on his own now.

I knew it was going to be a good morning as my feet

moved quietly down the paved road, which held a sheen of frost. I was headed to do the big loop to my secret spot, all the way around by the river and golf course. But something made me shift my route: I went directly off the road, down the driveway, along the edge of the Douglas fir and hemlock forest, and over to the meadow. I could not be out in the open because someone had just built a new house alongside the meadow. I didn't want to get caught trespassing and not be able to visit my spot in the meadow anymore. I had come so far with the animals there, and I couldn't risk it.

I walked softly, picturing the fox, picking up on any slight motion from the blurred edge of my vision like the owl. I sat next to the willow tree where I often saw the deer resting during the day. Sometimes I would find their tracks and the imprints they made when they lay in a bean shape in their daybed. As I sat down in their bed I smelled the grass, the trees, and the faint smell that the deer left behind when they last rested in that same place.

The sun came out and still I sat.

Just as I was getting restless and my stomach was starting to rumble with hunger, the first doe emerged from the shadows on the edge of the forest. There were four does walking gracefully. Calmly stopping mid-stride to look around for danger, they came out into the opening and continued into the meadow. They began to graze, pulling the grass with their mouths, reaching down, chewing their food as they walked. Very quietly, I got up from my spot next to the willow and started walking, lifting my legs high. My arms hung loose in front of me. I lifted and dropped my right hand as my left leg rose and fell, then did the same with my left hand and right leg, diagonally walking like the deer. I reached down with my mouth and bit a mouthful of grass and started chewing. My mind was not thinking of what my body was doing. It felt like the most natural thing in the world to be grazing there in the meadow with those does.

They started getting closer to me. I was making a conscious effort to slow my racing heart and frequently needed to close my eyes to calm the excitement building up inside. I made my way at an angle toward the trail they were moving along as I grazed, still walking through the grass like a doe. When I came to their trail a little way ahead of them, I paused beside it and hunched down in the tall grass, my body facing at a non-threatening angle away from the approaching does. One doe walked on the trail toward me, not noticing me. As she walked past, I slowly reached out my hand and she brushed against my fingertip. She flinched slightly and then continued on her way. She was so close I could hear her breath.

As she breathed out, I breathed in the same air.

Five tracking tips to take wherever you go, even your own backyard

My training as a wildlife tracker has helped me track wolves through the wilds of Alaska, mountain lions in California, and painted dogs through Botswana. These have all been life-changing experiences—but so is the time I spend on my own land using the same skills I use when tracking. You can approach any space, from a city street to a suburban yard to an old-growth forest, like a tracker—and your life will be full of awe and wonder. Spending time becoming aware of the nature around you is a great gift that brings you peace, contentment, and a sense of perspective about your connection to the world. Now it is time to lose your mind and come to your senses.

If you want to get the most out of your nature observation, use these tips:

CHOOSE A SPECIAL SPOT

Find a place near you where you feel closest to nature, and

commit to going there every day for a week (at least). This will allow you to start understanding the patterns of the animals around you—and the wildlife there will start getting used to you, too. Choose a spot that is easy to walk to. It could be in your own backyard, on a balcony with a container garden, or in a nearby park. At first you may not notice any wildlife, but as you begin to quiet your mind and body, you may begin to hear birdsong, notice feeding signs from a squirrel, or watch a bee land on a flower. When you are sitting, if you get restless focus on all of your five senses. Feel the ground beneath you, smell the air, listen to the quietest sound, taste the cool breeze, and look with the eyes of an owl.

WATCH WITH OWL EYES

Wild animals from songbirds to apex predators are acutely aware of the tiniest movement, including of your eyes, which means you need to stay as still as possible and use your peripheral vision if you don't want to alarm them. Watching with owl eyes means not moving your gaze at all—your eyes will stay in the same position. But you intentionally move your mind's focus to your peripheral vision. You won't see great detail with your peripheral vision, but you'll be able to pick up on even the subtlest movement, which will alert you to the presence of animals without scaring off the creatures you're trying to see. Try to see the ground, the sky, and as far to the left and right as you can without moving your eyes around. This will make your gaze non-threatening. Have you ever felt something and turned to see someone staring at you? You can practice this with a friend. Focus intently on the back of their head and see if they get uncomfortable. Then do it again, but this time instead of staring, go into your peripheral vision or owl eyes. When you go into owl eyes, your gaze is not threatening and your friend won't feel it the same way. You will find that nature will begin to accept you.

LISTEN WITH DEER EARS

Our ears are so overcome with human-made sounds that sometimes we don't hear the other sounds around us. There's a way to tune into the sounds of nature even when we think we're as far from nature as possible. Imagine that your ears are large like those of a mule deer, and listen for the very quietest sound you can hear. Listen for water flowing far away or the quiet chirp of a neighborhood songbird. Maybe there is a cicada buzzing in the distance, or snow landing on crinkled leaves. This is a way of tuning your ears to the sounds we normally ignore entirely. Eventually you may hear the soft swish of a beaver through the water, or the buzz of a hummingbird as it visits your balcony feeder.

WALK LIKE A FOX

Whether you're traveling to and from your special spot or just going for a stroll, practice your fox walk. The red fox has fine hairs growing in between the toes and heel pad of its feet, helping to buffer the sound of the footstep. The red fox also moves with a steady gait, head on a level plane, not bouncing up and down. This allows it to see subtle movements of mice as they scurry on the side of the trail. Set your feet down softly, the ball of your foot reaching forward to touch the earth, then slowly allow the rest of your foot to come down. Then, pulling your weight forward onto the ball as if you were feeling in the dark barefoot to avoid sharp, protruding objects, move silently.

USE YOUR INTUITION

You know that feeling when you come home expecting an empty house, but as soon as you walk inside you can sense someone else is there? Whether it's a "sixth sense" or just our subconscious picking up on signals our conscious mind ignores, we can tell when we're not the only human around. The more time you spend moving carefully through whatever nature is available to you, the more your intuition will expand to include non-human animals. Check in with yourself regularly to see whether you have a sense that you're not alone, and then use your owl eyes and deer ears to confirm your suspicion.

The more often you deliberately check in and immerse in your senses, the stronger those muscles will be, and the greater your understanding of the immense and magical web of life you live in.

Language of Nature

CHAPTER FIVE

I found myself sitting in a thick tangle of salmonberries. It was spring and all of the plants were so vibrant and lush that I felt intoxicated by the flush of new growth and the smells of buds bursting into a million shades of green. I had been learning tracking, and so far, I considered tracks to be prints on the ground, scat, or other signs such as territorial markings. In the two months since I'd shared breath with the deer, I'd learned to identify most of the tracks I came across and started to interpret the movement pattern and behavior based on what I was seeing on the ground. But here I was in the middle of a thicket, not sure exactly why—it just felt right. I reached my hand down and gently touched the depression in the ground with my fingertips. One, two, three, four, five toes in an arch and a large heel pad the size of my palm. I was still on the trail.

I had been tracking on Tiger Mountain, the tallest mountain in the highlands of Issaquah, with the group from WAS.

The founder of the school, Jon, and I were walking along in silence. I smelled the flowers that had just emerged from the red-flowering currant, the first sign of spring. The clusters bowed with the weight of the flowers, such a vibrant shade of pink and with a smell equally stimulating as the sight. The flowers were like a splash of paint in the wall of green that lay before me. Jon had signaled for me to look where he was looking. I did not recognize what I was seeing, a low tunnel in the thicket off to the side of the trail. He motioned for me to kneel down to the ground and peer in. I saw an arched tunnel just big enough for my body to move through. As I looked, my hand instinctively reached down to a depression in the ground. I felt an energy surge up through my arms and hands. The depression was big but I could not see the detail. He whispered "bear," and motioned for me to follow its path.

I found myself moving carefully down the tunnel, observing the tender spring shoots that surrounded me. I was hidden from the human trail in that bear tunnel and the branches were parting as my skin touched them, as if they had bent out of the way of a large body many times before. I moved on my hands and feet, rocking my head from side to side, lifting my nose to the air to smell the scents. My feet and hands rolled forward in an effortless, flowing stride. I continued through the tunnel, not always seeing the tracks, but continuing to feel electricity flowing up my limbs, a kind of numbness. Then I was there, in a thicket of salmonberry, with a smile from ear to ear. I was following something that had felt natural, instinctual, similar to when I encountered the deer.

From that moment on, I could not pass an animal trail without longing to follow that animal, to put myself in the body of the animal and attempt to see what it saw, move like it moved, and sense what it sensed. Tracks became alive to me, a strand that the animal left behind that would lead me to it and, I found, to a truer, wilder version of myself.

Learning the language of nature, learning what the birds and the snapped twigs and the whacking tails and the paw prints were communicating, reminded me of those words Macki Ruka spoke to me when I first learned of WAS. I was on the journey from my mind to my heart. When I trailed the bear I had followed my instincts, as if my body became the bear. As I continued to practice my tracking and wilderness survival, my mind would at times be the adversary to my instinct, losing the trail or worse yet, making mistakes because I did not follow my instincts. I wish I could say that my path to finding union with nature was a straight one, but it certainly wasn't.

The group of us at WAS often stayed overnight in shelters we built so we could be out in nature for as many hours of the day as possible. One day Rikki and I were determined to map the travel routes of all the wildlife we tracked on the sandbar of the Skykomish River. Rikki was a student of WAS, a couple years younger than I. She was a highly motivated homes-chooler who moved more like a wild animal than a person. Her brown hair was tied back in a ponytail and she wore the typical WAS outfit: khaki shorts and a fleece earth-tone shirt she made herself. Our plan was to stay overnight in the river valley so we could track on the sandbar from dawn to dusk.

The Skykomish River was a spot we frequented. When we went with WAS, we would show up in Chris's Suburban, track all day, and leave before all the mysteries were solved. We wouldn't come back until rain had washed the tracks away, and we had to start over with fresh mysteries. I had been looking forward to our trip, as I always enjoyed tracking with Rikki. She had a deep desire to engage in every moment playfully. I admired her lightness of spirit; she didn't seem bogged down with emotions. She had a youthfulness in her step and was always smiling. She had a knack for noticing the detail in everything we came across in nature, making her the perfect tracking companion.

We decided to each build our own survival shelter so we could stay there for a few days, waking up early and tracking all day until dark. We arrived at the sandbar in the morning and crossed over the railroad tracks to the forest on the edge of the vast riverbank. The enormous river valley led to the snow-peaked Cascade Range. After a day of tracking adventures, we started on our shelters. A hollowed-out cedar stump provided me a cocoon to fill with forest debris. I wove a door using the techniques I had learned from a basket weaver trained in the intricate art of Haida weaving, a simple over-and-under pattern originating from the center of crisscrossed saplings. I plugged the entrance with the woven insulated door and used moss and forest litter to fill in gaps. I tested it out; it was warm inside, with no drafts and very little room to move.

I went to check on Rikki's shelter. She was busily building her stick frame, which looked like a spine with ribs angled down toward the ground. The ridge pole was set in a notch of a tree and angled to the ground, leaving room under the pole for her to lie. I helped her gather up debris to pile on the outside. Dropping to my knees, I scraped up all the debris within arms' reach. Bigleaf maple, cottonwood, and alder leaves mixed with sticks and dirt piled up in front of me as I reached my arms around the stack, holding the pile against my body to carry over to the shelter. The sticks that angled from the top ridgepole to the ground stopped the debris from falling off.

Without hesitation, we started running to gather the debris, creating a game of speed and endurance. We each ran to a spot thick with debris and dropped to our knees to gather the largest pile we could carry. After running back, we plopped the debris on the outside, glancing at each other, rosy-cheeked and panting. Conjuring up the energy of the wolverine, whose power and tenacity overshadow their size, we persisted until the mound of debris stood as tall as us, stretching as wide around as it was high. After many trips collecting the material, I could reach my hand into the debris, working my fingers all the way to the spine, with the moist leaves reaching to my armpit. The thick insulation would keep Rikki warm, and if any rain were to fall it would shed off the outside layers before reaching the center where she would lie.

Exhausted from the day of tracking combined with the exertion of building our shelters, we put out the fire we had built to cook our food and headed to our respective homes for the night to dream of the tracking adventures of the day.

The ringing sound of metal on metal was gaining on me. I heard the train horn, a loud forlorn howl in the night. The clanking of the couplings and the low rumble of the engine were so close. I needed to break free from the shackles. I felt the cold train tracks below me. I had no time to ponder how I had gotten into this predicament. I only knew I must get out of it, off the tracks to safety before being flattened like the pennies I had set on the tracks as a child. I conjured up all of the strength I had inside of me as the ripple of the vibration from the train came at me like an earthquake. I was wrapped up tight and weighted down. I could not move my arms or my legs. I screamed, pushed and kicked, wriggled and jolted. My eyes could not pierce the darkness. As my adrenaline surged, my heart raced. I found a spot that gave way to my force. Leaves flying, moss and sticks covering my body and the ground around me, I sat outside my log with the distant sound of the train echoing through the valley.

I sat up all night shivering because I'd destroyed my shelter due to fears conjured up in my dreamtime. Rikki emerged at dawn fully rested from the night, and I lay in a ball with heaps of debris loosely piled on my cold skin in an attempt to blanket myself with the earth. I knew I had a long way to go before all parts of me were comfortable in the wild.

As my time went on at WAS, my fellow students and I continued to develop our understanding of nature language as well as our own group communication, which often happened nonverbally because we were paying attention to the sounds of nature. We all had specific roles to play within the group. One role was to make sure everyone was paying attention at all times. Our classmate Justin typically took on this role, and he would sneak around, hide on the path in front of us, and scare us as we walked past.

The group of us would go out and sit around a pond the school had named *Linne Doran*, Gaelic for Pond of the Otter. We each had our own spot, our territory. The pond was large, with a beaver dam slowing the water as it exited downstream.

We learned every square inch of that pond. From where we sat we drew a circle on a map with each of us in the center of our own circle. Each circle touched the ones on either side. This was our territory. This was to ensure that no place was overlooked when we went and sat to record all of the bird language and other observations surrounding the pond.

We students developed a series of calls that we used to signify certain things as we were out at our territorial spots. The great horned owl call—a low rhythmic muffled *whoo-who-who-whodo-who*—meant to leave the area unnoticed. The loud flicker's *clear!* would signify to run back to our meeting spot. A third call, the chickadee's *chickadee-dee-dee,* meant to walk back at our baseline, or natural relaxed pace, not disturbing any birds or wildlife as we moved. Wolf howls, raven calls, and jay alarms were all part of our code.

Our meeting spot, *Malalo Ya Chui,* which is Akamba for Lair of the Leopard, was named by one of the elder advisors of the school, Ingwe. As a young boy from British ancestry, Ingwe was attended to by an Akamba tribesman and spent time by his village fires in Kenya. Our meeting spot had eight sides, a dirt floor and a roof to keep the rain off. Inside this structure we mapped out in detail each of our observations from our time at the pond. Our notes read like this: *Winter wren bullet alarm, joined by another four or five feet off the ground with beak facing down. Single kinglet alarm as Terry enters his territory. Steller's jay sneak call. Blue heron moved—doing mating dance. Ruby-crowned kinglet moving east from Greg's spot. Female hooded mergansers swimming in middle of pond. Raven calling. Kinglets getting louder* cee-cee-cee *call. Winter wren song above Rikki. Tree frog chorus begins—pileated woodpecker flew overhead calling.* We assigned each of these observations a number and letter and placed them on the map in sequential order according to the time frame and location during which they occurred.

If there was something out of the ordinary, like an alarm or a sudden flight from a group of birds, we would go investigate. In the case of the two winter wrens alarming with their beaks facing down, for example, we visited the exact spot we'd heard them and found the small imprints of a long-tailed weasel.

We then developed extensive acronyms for each of the observations we started to experience on a regular basis: OAF, owl approaches forest. WWA, winter wren alarm. GBHL, great blue heron lands. BCLPP, bobcat licking private parts. (Actually, that last code was one we were always hoping to observe, but we never did. It was nevertheless included in all of our map keys.)

It was easy to tell if one of the students was distracted or if there was a human intruder in our vicinity by how the birds responded. We sat one afternoon at each of our designated territories. The birds were used to our presence now, and continued with their typical behavior of feeding, interjecting an occasional lazy afternoon song or call. Suddenly, there began a wave of bird alarms from the east that came closer and closer. The birds were fleeing as if for their lives. I could see the other students looking in the direction of the alarms. I stood up as the birds around me started to fly away. I wondered if there was something I should be running from. Just then a man in tall waders with a fishing pole slung over his shoulder crossed the dam at the outlet of the pond. His head faced the ground and he was walking swiftly, without so much as pausing to look at the beauty of his surroundings. The man was oblivious to the birds flushing out of their core territory, fleeing from the danger as if a giant monster that had the power to kill them and their families was approaching. I recognized this as a sign of a human not belonging. The bird language gave us a glimpse into the effect of all of our actions.

Once I realized I too was causing alarms, I started to do something about it. When I first came to WAS and learned about bird language, I began by just walking slowly, paying attention to every sound and movement around me. In the beginning of the heightened observation I noticed that the birds still stopped singing and flew off to safety. Then it got to the point where I could catch the birds off guard, like the time I saw the song sparrow feeding on the ground on the trail in front of me just before she fled to safety, alarming to the rest of the species. With the intentional practice of awareness and many attempts to walk through the forest without setting off the warning signs of wildlife, I eventually got to the point where I could consistently walk under a singing bird without that bird so much as pausing in song, and only then was I able to get close to wildlife like I had at my secret spot. I sensed the language of nature going on all around me. I sensed the freedom from the confines of form, structure, and law, like the clouds moving into an area and moving out—part of the unfolding of all life. This awareness came from the silence.

I learned to listen for the silence between the notes of a great horned owl's call or the pause of a ruby-crowned kinglet as it landed on the ground to feed. When in the silence, I transcended fears and doubt and felt only happiness and connection to nature. Nothing but that moment in time existed.

It was this inner quietness that we brought into our scout game, the culmination of our training at the end of the school year and a test of how well we had learned the language of nature. Our group started attending the scout camp my second year at WAS. After two years of wilderness immersion, this was the first time I brought my skills to a competition outside our little group of teenagers. In the northeastern corner of Washington, we were to compete amongst the world's greatest trainees in stealth and survival in a scout game put on by Coyote Path Wilderness School.

My classmates and I were nervous; we were going into a region we didn't know. We were intimately familiar with every bird, every animal trail, in our own territory. We were worried about whether our skills would even apply in a new region, especially since some of our adversaries knew the region well. We thought for sure they would be able to evade the birds by knowing all of their territories like we were able to do back at our pond.

The group we were up against were masters in martial arts and stealth and experts in camouflage and hunting. Some of them were former members of Special Operations Forces. Then there was the group of us, barefoot, at least ten years younger than anyone there. Glenn Morris, a legendary ninja master, was leading part of the pre-game training. We practiced mind control by walking on hot coals. We studied camouflage patterns that fit into the surrounding plants and trees. Then we had a chance to study the plants themselves and which ones were good for food or fire. When the game was about to begin, each person was given five marbles, a bag of potatoes, and a tin can. We were then divided into four teams with distinguished territories around a large pond. My team consisted of other students from WAS. The other teams assembled themselves based on varying strengths so the teams would be well rounded. At least we had one advantage over these experts—we all knew each other and were used to communicating silently in the wilderness. To say we were intimidated would be an understatement. As we looked at the other teams, professionals in this type of stealth, we felt we had bitten off more than we could chew. We were to make fire by friction to boil and purify our water, harvest wild edibles, and live like traditional Indigenous scouts. We had to stay out of sight to everyone outside our team. If we caught someone, we would take a marble from them. The person with the most marbles won the game. If someone had all of their marbles taken, they were out of the game.

Each team also had a flag within their territory. We had to find the location of the other teams' flags without being seen, and on the last night we planned to raid the other teams' camps. The teams that got their flag stolen would lose the game. No one knew which team would be planning an ambush on which flag.

On the second day out, Rikki and I went to find the location of the other teams' flags while Justin and Greg stayed at camp guarding ours. They lay in wait, camouflaged amongst leaf litter to catch any intruding teams, while Rikki and I tried to find the exact location of all the other flags so we could make a plan for their capture in the darkness. We traveled silently, using the base of a hill for cover, going from tree to tree. Up the hill a spotted towhee came out from the grass and sounded an alarm, then a dark-eyed junco joined in. A song sparrow alarmed. The birds were like popcorn popping up out of the grass and pine scrub. Rikki and I looked at each other, nodded, then each found a spot to hide. I crouched down behind a mound of dirt and pine needles. She stood behind a tree. The alarms continued, getting louder and closer. We stayed silent, knowing that there was someone approaching our hiding places. I had already seized five marbles from unsuspecting opposing team members and Rikki had close to that amount. We spent a full two minutes in hiding, listening to the popping of bird alarms rolling down the hill, grateful that the birds alarmed for so long before the arrival of an intruder. Out of the brush, in full camouflage, face painted to match the bronze earth, he finally appeared. He was quiet in the woods, did not make a sound as he crouched low in the brush. I could tell he had trained in stealth; he was possibly one of the Special Operations Forces that we were up against. When he arrived within earshot of me, I whispered, "I see you." He jumped with a look of shock and begrudgingly reached into his pocket to pull out a marble and hand it over. The perturbed look of a middle-aged man getting outsmarted by a teenager was priceless. Rikki continued to lie hidden, out of sight. The man never knew there were two of us. The birds had come through, and all the alarms we had learned from our forest transferred to the scout camp. Different birds, different territories, but the same patterns.

We survived. We cooked our potatoes and cattails on a smokeless fire we made by using very small dry sticks and keeping the fire hot. Justin captured the other teams' flags in the silence of night while the rest of us perched around the pond, keeping guard. On the final morning, when the howl of the wolf called us in, marking the end of the game, we counted all our marbles. I had the most, with Rikki close behind. The legendary Glenn Morris, who had traveled the world training with Japanese ninja warriors, commented that our group was made up of the most peaceful and quiet-minded individuals he had ever met. He was amazed at how we could move through the forest so quietly, like animals. What truly set us apart that week from others just as comfortable in the wilderness was our ability to listen and use our senses to interpret the animals around us.

After scout camp we went back to our routine of gathering at Malalo Ya Chui, where we learned to internalize the language of nature. Bonded from the scout camp as a team, we stayed overnight in the hut in the cedar forest, and we danced in celebration. Around a fire we moved as animals. Rikki, Terry, Michael, Justin, Greg, and I all moved as our own individual animal. We each had our own dance in the darkness with only the flicker of the flame as light, the sound of raindrops on the roof, and the beat of a rawhide drum. Wild, brave Justin danced the mountain lion and stalked Rikki, who danced the deer. Greg moved as the wolverine and Terry as the weasel. The flames moved as we moved and we all entered into a place where the flame rises and disappears into the invisible. I danced the wolf. I pictured the animal so undiluted that my body became the wolf. I realized that like the wolf, we leave a mark on the great tapestry of life with each step we take. Those marks may be washed away by time, but the language of nature is never forgotten.

Lone Wolf

CHAPTER SIX

My first year of Wilderness Awareness School and the time I spent alone at my secret spot had given me so much. But I didn't feel I knew enough. Rather, I knew just enough to know I had much more to learn. Prior to the scout competition, I searched for my place amongst the wild creatures. The animal that brought me closest in my journey to my heart was the wolf.

In the spring of 1997, my first year at WAS, I went to live and work on an organic farm in the Snoqualmie Valley. I traveled to the Wilderness Awareness School during the week, and worked on the farm on weekends, harvesting for the first Community Supported Agriculture program in the region. My mother was relieved that I had found a place nearby with a nice young couple who were starting the first organic farm in the region. Sprite and Chantal came and went as they continued to travel the circuit of rainbow gatherings, festivals, and concerts. I was a little tempted to go along as I had the year before; I knew that despite how much I liked the farm work, I wasn't ready to settle in one place yet. But getting a taste of real nature awareness had been like tasting a ripe apricot for the first time, and I knew I wouldn't get more of it on the road with Sprite and Chantal. As summer approached and WAS would be taking a break, I decided it was time to leave the farm for a while and head out on another adventure.

I caught wind of a bluegrass festival that was happening in Talkeetna, Alaska, so I made plans to go north in hopes of finding people living closer to the earth. Now sixteen, I was equipped with my driver's license and a white VW Golf that my oldest sister, Serene, had given me after she graduated college. I headed north from the farm in Snoqualmie at the beginning of the summer. Leaving my car in Vancouver, I hopped on a ferry over to Vancouver Island. Here I was sure to find people who were living off the land! Free from my car, I caught a ride with some friends I met on the mainland side. My first destination was a secluded beach on the west coast of the island. Keeha Beach was a place where new hippie types gathered, camped, and lived out amongst wild nature. Nights were filled with campfires, music, and chanting, and the days were spent swimming in the ocean and having long talks and walks on the beach. Though it seemed idyllic, I was unsettled. My journey was so different from that of the carefree people living on the beach. I felt more kinship to animals I tracked than I did with people at that point in my life.

While camping there I dreamed of tracking a white female wolf, tracking more than just her footprints in the ground. I was tracking what her body language was saying as she stood looking at me, shaking her head. She seemed like she was struggling inside. The dream flashed back to the summer before, when I was caught beside a river that night in Colorado and lost something so dear to me. Anger and despair raged inside me as the dream shifted back to the wolf. She was still standing, staring at me. She shifted her weight from side to side, as if she were deciding whether she wanted to flee. Just then, a white swan landed in a pond close to the wolf. The wolf glanced over, stood taller, and slowly walked away. I followed her, not noticing the details of her tracks, but knowing instinctually where to go. The wolf went into a cave. I followed. Suddenly I became the wolf inside the den, surrounded by my family of wolves.

The next morning I awoke early, the only image in my mind that white wolf. I knew she was real, out there somewhere. I packed up my tent and sleeping bag in the darkness and slipped out on the trail to head north and find the wolf from my dream. I felt as if there were a pulsing umbilical cord connected to me, guiding me, and the source that fed the cord was the wolf. First I had to gather up some supplies. Packing up my warm jacket, some freeze-dried food, nuts, a pot and an extra pair of shoes into my pack, I had everything I needed in case there was no place to stop and restock on my journey.

I began hitchhiking north. The first person who picked me

up was a logger, one of the people I saw as responsible for the decimation of old-growth cedar forests occurring in the area. But he revealed a deep reverence for the land, and I quickly realized that the problem lay with a lack of ecological perspective in the logging companies.

The next person I rode with was a woman named Angie. She was older and looked like a modern-day witch with her jet-black hair that moved wildly as she turned her head to greet me with a huge smile. There were crystals, stones, and beads on the dash of her car and the sweet aromatic smell of sage permeated my seat. She seemed to have a strong intuition of my character from the way she looked at me, studying my eyes and body language. Our meeting reminded me of two ravens perched together on a tree, heads bobbing, bodies moving from side to side, chattering away in our own distinctive tone. She invited me for dinner and to stay the night before continuing my journey to Port Hardy the next day. I took her up on her offer. She took me to a beach where we went digging for trade beads. She had a large collection of beads that had originally come from islands off the coast of Russia and had been traded to the natives for pelts. The beads were beautiful amber, cobalt, and gold. I kept some in my pocket throughout my journey for good luck and prosperity.

The next night I camped close to the ferry terminal at Port Hardy, aiming to catch the seven-thirty morning ferry to Prince Rupert, a port city on a coastal island of British Columbia. When I awoke, I climbed up a Douglas fir tree and sighted my first orcas out in the bay. I watched as a long-tailed weasel ran in and out of the logs along the forest's edge. I took all this as a good sign. I was nearly out of money and I was hoping to weasel my way onto the ferry.

And I did, by luck and wit. I found a nice young woman with an old hatchback Volvo and I hid under blankets in her back seat as she drove through the terminal. I rode the ferry through the Inside Passage, past waterfalls and mountains. The wilderness looked untouched by humans, with no roads or houses. There was only the occasional boat docked on the shore. I had the urge to jump off the boat and disappear into the wild forever. After arriving and spending a rainy night in Prince Rupert, I hit the road early the next morning. I found numerous folks eager to give me rides on the long highway. After ten hours on the road, I walked off the side of the Alaska Highway somewhere close to the border of Yukon Territory. I was tired and looked forward to being in my tent in the woods alone. I wanted to let my guard down. I had been immensely aware of every move of each driver, always ready to ditch it if things got strange. But once camped I still couldn't let my guard down because I was in grizzly country with only my backpack. I hung my backpack up in a tree away from my tent and put some clean clothes on, hoping I could keep the smells of food out of my tent. I drifted off into an edgy sleep, waking to the slightest sounds outside.

The next day I made it to the Alaskan border. The rides were long, fortunately; not many people traveled short distances in those parts and the daylight hours lengthened as I headed north. There was so much to look at out the windows. I saw large lakes with swans swimming in them, reminding me of my wolf dream. I saw clear-cuts and the dense plantations of forests cultivated after the land was stripped of the old-growth cover.

A biologist named Jim drove me over the Alaskan border. I had all kinds of questions to ask him, and especially wanted to know about the wolves. He knew the packs in the area and referred to them with their pack names. He knew the biologists who were responsible for locating, collaring, and naming the wolf packs. With rugged terrain, shifting pack territories, and long travel distances, the wolves in that area are difficult to study. The radio collars, typically attached to the alpha members of the pack, provide useful data for research. He said they were thriving in northern British Columbia nearby and that if I was headed for Denali I was sure to see some up close in the wild. Just then I saw movement on the road ahead. Jim raced the Subaru station wagon up the road just in time to see a grey wolf dart down a trail off the side of the road. He pulled the car over and we jumped out. The wolf, in all its grandeur, emerged once again, striding across the open plain. It glanced back at us briefly before loping off into the tundra, which still looked hardened by incessant winter nights. It wasn't my white wolf, but it was the first time I'd seen a wolf in the wild, and I was thrumming with a feeling of recognition and destiny.

Jim dropped me at a parking lot by a grocery store and

hotel. He gave me money to call my mom on a payphone.
I could tell he was worried, being a father himself. I walked
over to the payphone, and as I picked up the phone to dial, he
drove away. Then I slowly set the plastic handle back on the
metal bracket. I didn't know what to say to my mother, whom
I had left again. Should I tell her I had abandoned the car and
taken off alone into the deep wilderness? I decided she was
better off not knowing. It wasn't until I became a mother myself that I realized how cavalier I had been.

I made my way to Denali, abandoning the idea of the bluegrass festival in Talkeetna in favor of finding the white wolf. I
listened to a tutorial in the ranger station on what to do if I
encountered a grizzly bear (which would have been helpful
to know before I was camping in grizzly country), and then
I asked about the wolf packs. On a large topographic map, a
ranger pointed out the river valleys where the specific packs
lived. Thrilled to have an idea of their territory, I hopped on
a green bus to head out into the national park wilderness.
Denali was a land of mountains and glaciers. Rivers braided
through valleys silted from the glacial melt of spring. A single
road led into Denali National Park. Apart from the road and a
few scattered campgrounds, the wilderness looked untouched
by humans. In awe of the surrounding mountains awaiting
exploration, I was anxious to get off the bus.

When we neared the Teklanika River, one of the places a
pack had recently been seen feeding on a bull caribou, I sat up
in my seat, scanning the river valley, then shouted for the bus

driver to stop. I'd seen a group of people tracking on a river-bank. Unbelievably, it was my friends from WAS. I gathered up my gear, hopped off the bus, and headed toward the bridge and my friends.

They were awestricken as I walked up with my Osprey backpack and a knitted hat pulled over my dreadlocks. They had last seen me over a month earlier, before everyone headed out on their summer adventures. I'd said that I was hitting the road and I was not sure where I was going or when I would see them next. Yet there I was, standing in the Denali wilder-ness on the rocky bank of the Teklanika River. I was relieved to have camaraderie.

Anne was there, which I found comforting. I was still re-belling against my poor mother, separating myself from her to form my own identity, but I could talk to Anne, having spent all that time with her as one of the quiet mentors facilitating my connection to the earth at WAS. She had told me earlier that she'd be going to Alaska for a wolf-tracking expedition, but she hadn't told me exactly where, and at any rate I'd dis-missed it, not wanting to make any firm plans but rather to follow my instincts instead. Those instincts guided me right there, meeting up with the WAS group the same day they'd arrived. Even before setting up camp, they'd gone out to scout wolf tracks on the riverbank, just as my bus had gone by.

I soaked up as much tracking knowledge as I could. Almost two weeks after I'd met up with the WAS crew, I woke early to head out alone on the trail. I kept to the wildlife paths and quickly picked up on a fresh trail of a wolf. Often the human trails would intersect, joining or running parallel to the wild-life trails for a distance and then branching off again. I wanted to internalize this wolf's trail, which was so defined that it looked as though generations of wolves had passed along it, uninhibited by change brought about by humans.

It was also here on the trail where I first heard the call of the wolf, so strong it permeated into my body like a warm-ing embrace after a sad cry. It was the distinctive howl of a lone wolf, a call that seemed to drag on, trailing off toward the end before disappearing into the silence. That howl took hold of me and a kinship emerged between the wolf and me. Far from my home, I was able to let self-doubt, distractions, and old patterns drift off with the wind. The feeling from my dream of being the wolf and entering the den with my family was becoming a reality as I stood on the wolf trail connecting with the tracks. I reached down to the side of the trail to eat a cloudberry, still tart and unripe. I scanned the area around me. And then suddenly there she was. A lone white wolf running across the side of a tundra-covered hill. The wolf who had been calling to me, who'd come to me in my dream. The wolf lived and thrived there. I wanted to learn from her, move with her grace and feel a part of a pack.

I continued on in the direction of the wolf—my wolf. I ran barefoot amongst the deep, soft arctic and caribou moss. I had seen only a glimpse of her and I wanted to get closer, follow her. I followed the tracks, longing to catch up to her and see her up close. Running with the moist air against my face, I felt a sharp pain in my toe. I crumpled to the ground, discovering that a bearberry branch had been broken off, exposing a sharpened stick that had impaled my foot. My humanness shook me out of my trance of running down the wolf trail. I limped back to camp, bleeding.

On my way back to camp I felt the throbbing up into my foot. The seriousness of my puncture wound was setting in. I would need to let myself heal before reattempting my meeting with the wolf. The expedition would soon come to an end, and I was not sure how I would hitchhike down the Alaska Highway back to my car in the shape I was in. Anne gave me her plane ticket back to Seattle, and she rode home with the camp cook.

I was torn as I approached the airport. I had Anne's driver's license in hand, equipped with her social security number and mother's maiden name, and I was so grateful for her help in getting home after my injury. But I had left something unfinished in the wilderness of Alaska. I needed to learn more from the wolves.

Leaving Denali, I was also leaving behind my constant companion since I was thirteen years old: the urge to run away. It turned out I'd only been running from myself, and the anguish I had caused my family was now reflecting back at me. I had thought at that time I would go back to Denali and see that wolf again, but I soon realized that she had taught me what I need to learn from her, one of my biggest lessons in life. I had developed an instinctual empathy toward each person within the tracking expedition, and I began to see how I had to face the hurt I had caused my family, especially my mother. My longing to spend more time with the wolf pack was no longer about running away from something, but rather running toward what I felt in the wilderness. I learned from the white wolf that my time as a lone wolf had come to an end. She led me to join my pack, just as she had in my dream.

Pack

CHAPTER SEVEN

February 18, 1998
Fall City, Washington
Clear sky all through the night waxing half moon,
sunrise 7:12 a.m., sunset 5:35 p.m. 45 degrees.

B*eautiful sunrise over the mountains. Low fog in the valley below. While I climbed up to the top of a cedar tree this morning, the first bird was a winter wren alarming. There was a series of alarms from two different individuals. I heard the later one of them singing. A pileated woodpecker landed five feet from my tree and began to feed. I could see the red crest above stripes of white and black on the head and the patch of red at the base of the beak. It must have been an adult male. When he was pecking at the dead wood of a standing alder, his body looked completely black below the neck. I could see the white under his wings when they lifted up in flight. I loved the feeling I got when this creature was near. He reminded me of how important it is to be thankful for all of the species* *on earth. His relative the ivory-billed woodpecker no longer appears in field guides due to the destruction of the old-growth forests of the Southeast. I hope that will never be the case for the pileated.*

I saw so many birds this morning from my tree: winter wren, Bewick's wren, ruby-crowned kinglet, black-capped chickadee, white-breasted nuthatch, pileated woodpecker, hairy woodpecker, spotted towhee, dark-eyed junco, American robin, Steller's jay, crow, red-tailed hawk, hooded merganser, Canada goose, and song sparrow.

I went tracking today at the Skykomish River sandbar with WAS. It was raining. There are a lot of bear trails all over leading to the river where all the salmon are. It was so much fun tracking the bear, seeing the claws of where a bear had stepped up a steep hill, slipping in the mud. So much power in these tracks. Before we went out we all set the intention that no trees would fall on us. A lot of trees have been coming down lately. A huge cottonwood fell just minutes after we had been under it and it made a huge crash. I could feel the earth shake. I gathered willows to make a basket that evening. I practiced fire in the rain. I had a bigleaf maple for a spindle, a cedar for a board, and a rock as a handhold for my bowdrill. It glazed over and barely smoked. I need to work more on my fire.

I am striving to have 100 percent awareness of everything around me. I need to put my whole self into things. I know it is old patterns coming up that are preventing me from doing so. I need to stay in the positive mind and not get bogged down with self-doubt. I need to do a vision quest or something so I can work through these struggles.

Passion inside me

I release and become wild

When my heart is full
I become a wolf.

I resolved that I would continue to soak up the wisdom
of the wolves. I read everything I could about them: research
papers, books, and stories. Occasionally there would be wolf
sightings in Washington State, though they were understood to
have been nonexistent there since the last documented breeding pair in the 1930s (Moskowitz 2013). I would follow up
on any sightings, getting glimpses of the tracks from unknown
packs or lone wolves passing through the rugged North Cascades. But the packs never stayed very long; humans loomed
too close.

After the Alaska trip, I continued to learn from the wolves
firsthand every summer. In the summer of 1998, I traveled in
the remote wilderness of Idaho. I worked as a wildlife tracker with the Wilderness Awareness School as they continued
their wolf-tracking expeditions in the Frank Church–River
of No Return Wilderness, which is within the largest tract
of wilderness in the lower forty-eight states. A group of us
who were trained as trackers led adults who signed up for the
expedition to learn tracking and wolf ecology and to immerse
in the wilderness. We taught them the basics of track and
sign—how to identify the tracks, scat, and markings we came
across. We guided the groups through an experience much like

many of our days in Washington with WAS, taking long treks to experience the wilderness through the eyes of the wolf. We also interacted with researchers who were studying the pack behavior and collected data that could be used in their studies.

As a keystone species, wolves taught me not only about themselves, but also about the whole interwoven ecosystem. By tracking the wolf I was also tracking the smallest shrew, the herds of elk, the badgers, the ravens. Wolf kills provide a windfall for other species. The remains are pilfered by an array of carnivores—four-legged, two-legged, and many-legged (Wilmers et al. 2003). Plant life also thrives with healthy wolf populations. The pack-hunting predators keep the ungulates, or hoofed mammals, out in the grasslands, where they can see an approaching wolf pack. This takes pressure off the woodland and riparian areas (wetlands adjacent to rivers and streams) and keeps the grasses that evolved with grazing animals vibrant. When wolves are present in a system, the interlocking food web is complete. Predators, prey, and plants form the levels of the food web. The predators are indirectly helping the plants (Ripple and Beschta 2012). Thus riparian areas thrive, resulting in an increase in the right kind of habitat for beavers and songbirds.

I tracked. Often I would be dropped off alone at first light on a fresh track with just a water bottle and a radio. I would follow the tracks, sometimes until I found the animal. That was a true reward of the tracking experience—getting to track all the way to the animal. The tracks weren't usually fresh enough for me to catch up to the animal who'd left them, but when I spotted fresh tracks, everything else fell away and it was just the trail and me. My body fell into rhythm with life around me, and the earth became a series of mysteries unraveling before me. I imagined it was waking in my brain the patterns of hunter-gatherers.

When I was in the Frank Church Wilderness in 2001, I was following the tracks of an alpha wolf. In that central section of wilderness there were sheepherders who came seasonally while the weather was good; the Idaho grasses provided plenty of forage for large flocks of sheep. The herders, on horseback and with dogs, moved the sheep through the grassy meadows. At night they stayed in wagon tents covered with canvas while their Great Pyrenees stood as watchdogs outside.

I always wondered what it would be like to be a sheepherder. I imagined myself out on a horse, keeping watch over the large flocks of livestock and moving slowly through vast landscapes of mountains, rivers, and meadows. The sheep left dusty trails through the wilderness as they traveled from one feeding ground to the next. They moved in a line, the ones behind stepping in the trail of the ones in front for the path of least resistance. Were the sheep following those wildlife trails and wearing them in, or were the elk, bear, and coyotes shifting their trails to follow a well-worn path left behind by the sheep being herded to a new lush meadow next to a meandering stream? Either way, the worn-in dusty sheep trails made early morning tracking in the fine dust a fruitful endeavor: the wolves followed the trails too, because they were an easy way to travel long distances without going through a deadfall of limbs, tall grasses, and rocky hillsides.

About halfway through the expedition in mid-August, I got dropped off partway into the morning scout patrol, the first-light run to find any fresh tracks that had been laid the previous night. The scout, the one who goes to find the fresh tracks, sets the plan for the day by choosing the most likely place to bring the groups of trackers. We started out that morning as a group of the lead trackers on the expedition, and I was ready if I needed to be dropped off while the rest of the trackers went back to camp to prepare the groups for the day. We had rigged up a seat on the front of a Ford F250 truck, and one tracker would sit there while other trackers would stand on the running boards hanging over the side, watching for fresh trails.

Prior to making the drive, we sat at camp in the darkness, drinking our tea and looking again at the topographical maps showing where we had seen the wolf pack in the days leading up to this one. Based on patterns we'd documented, we tried to predict where the wolves were going and where we were most likely to pick up on their fresh track. We followed the main road for a long distance, out toward Interstate 21 and the town of Stanley, and made a turn back north up a less-used route toward a backcountry horse camp. Getting as close to the predicted territory borders as possible, we hoped to find tracks of the alpha male going on scout patrol himself, marking along boundaries by leaving scent through scat and urine as a communication to other dominant wolves in that region. Following the tracks of the alpha would give us a better picture of the territory of the pack. The role of the alpha is to be the wisest animal, able to keep the pack alive by avoiding conflict with other wolf packs. A common cause of death for wolves is from other wolves at a territory boundary. The tracks of the alpha would help to paint the picture of where the pack will travel so as to not trespass into another pack's territory.

Standing on the running board, my knuckles white from my grip on the passenger side of the truck, I shivered from the cold mountain air driving into me at thirty miles per hour. Suddenly I saw them—perfect tracks in a straight line. I motioned for the driver to stop. This moment was the widening of a tributary of my life, where the stream of tracking became a river rushing toward the larger current of my journey.

In the fine dust on the edge of the road were tracks with four large toes, each with a sharply pointed claw accentuating the toes like a dot on a lowercase *i*. The negative space between the toes and the heel pad formed a star-like shape where the muscles in the foot nearly pulled the earth up as the foot departed the ground. I examined the two tracks, the rear paw landing directly on the place the front paw had pressed first. The next pair of tracks was twenty-seven inches in front of the first two. Our group moved silently, each inspecting a different part of the trail. One tracker was hunched down, looking at the detail of the perfectly placed track in the dust.

Another tracker squatted down to the height of the wolf, peering down the trail to see what the animal had seen when traveling this route.

Studying the trail, I placed my hand just over each set of two tracks up in the air, moving it slightly from left to right in a rhythm as my gaze moved slightly left and right with the trail. I was internalizing the cadence of the wolf. Stripping off my outer clothes, I signaled to my friends that I was going to head off alone. I pulled out the map to look in the direction of the tracks. We chose a place several miles away to meet. If I was not there by 4:00 p.m., I was to find a high point to get in radio contact at that time. I was wearing shorts, a T-shirt, and leather shoes with thin soles. I had a radio strapped to my left hip and a water bottle strapped to my right. In my pocket were a small notebook and pencil, a knife, and a miniature tape measure. As I left the group they began dissecting a scat, which was blackish, the color signifying a feeding on nutrient-rich organ meat. The alpha pair feast on the organ meat following a pack's kill before any of the other pack members begin to eat. The scat was left at a prominent trail crossing just before the wolf had made a turn to cross over the river.

I followed the tracks along a large mountain meadow bounded by dense lodgepole pine forest. As I ran I scared up a pair of sandhill cranes, and the majestic, tall migratory birds called as they flew, sounding an eerie echo. When the sheep trail went over a small mountain, the wolf tracks followed. I inclined toward a hilltop, welcoming the drops of rain that had begun falling softly on my face. I continued jogging, one hand out in front of me, palm facing downward, moving slightly from left to right to match the patterns in the wolf trail. The horizon lay ahead: I could now see the tops of the trees as the elevation dropped beyond the peak of the summit in front of me.

The rain only lasted until I reached the apex. I paused at the summit, taking in my surroundings through all of my senses. I knelt down to investigate the track. The print was clear and alive. It was as if the substrate was still looking for a place to settle from the disturbance of the paw. The particles of dust were suspended on the crest of the negative space between the toes, anticipating the elements of wind allowing them to descend the ridges into the valley left by the pads. Surrounding the unblemished wolf track were drops of rain. With this cognition my body became a conduit of electricity. I could feel my heart racing and my fingers and toes going numb. The tracks had landed *on top* of the rain that had fallen just five minutes before.

I glanced along the trail toward the decline in both directions. One would take me toward the wolf, the other back down the trail. I brought the image of the topographic map to mind, searching it for this spot. I recalled that the green forested hills of the map showed wavy lines that were close together, signifying steeper, higher terrain. I followed the hills downward with my mind's eye and the wavy lines grew wider, spreading out as the elevation descended, eventually coming to a valley shown in white with a meandering creek depicted in blue traveling through the center. Winding along the creek valley on the map were dark dotted lines depicting roads. I recalled the road that led to the valley I was approaching, where I planned to meet the truck again. It was nearing high noon and with the meeting time at four o'clock, I calculated the miles and time it would take me to arrive at the meeting spot. I had to continue.

The wolf was so close now. I felt as if I were floating, gliding along the trail in the zone of the wolf. I was disconnected from the limitations of my own physical body. I felt I could run a hundred miles and not tire. My footsteps fell silently on the dust as I slowed my stride to a walk. Approaching the place where the edge of the forest met the open meadow, I paused before stepping out from the shadows of the trees. The sun was directly overhead. In that moment I stood frozen in my tracks next to the fresh footprint of the wolf that had led me here. I was sharing this trail with the wolf and I did not want the moment to end. I wanted that wolf to be with me forever.

I was learning the detail of his tracks, his stride, the way he turned his head while on the trail to follow his senses, being led by his dominant sense of smell. Through his tracks I had seen the way he paused at a protuberance of a stump to leave his scent. Stopping, lifting a hind leg up high to urinate, he conveyed a complex message that lasted long after he passed. I saw his dedication when he was in his own baseline trot, the speed at which the wolf mostly travels, covering that long distance like an arrow released from a bow. I knew I would carry that moment I spent alone with the wolf on the sheep trail in the mountains into my life.

I moved slowly out into the meadow opening, glancing back toward the forest edge. The meadow was large and curved to match the undulating creek. I could not see the expanse even as I stepped out into the open because of its horseshoe shape. I paused. I caught a movement out of the corner of my eye. It was a dark wolf moving with effortless grace just inside the forest's edge. Then it was gone. I peered closely, squinting, but did not see the wolf again.

Approaching the valley floor, the feeling I'd been experiencing that I had transcended the physical constraints of my body dissipated. My feet ached and my body shook from the exertion of my morning. I took off my shoes and walked down the bank of a cold mountain stream that wove a meandering pathway through the lush meadow. I sank my toes in, then submerged to my knees, lying with my back on the smooth rocks of the stream bank. The image of the wolf moving on the forest periphery continued to replay in my mind when I closed my eyes.

Lying there exhausted, I suddenly heard a howling in the direction I had just come from. Then another howl started to my left, and another to my right. An entire pack erupted in howling. I could hear younger wolves sounding a higher-pitched howl interspersed with yipping, their voices cracking like a teenage boy's, joining the low drone of the adult wolves. Each howl was distinct, and together they formed a group harmony, a family chorus. All of the hair on the back of my neck stood up straight. As the howling died down I wondered why this chorus had erupted. It was the time of year for the pack to be rearing pups, which could have been why they were howling—to keep track of all the members of the pack. Or possibly there was a kill site nearby and there was still food to be feasted on.

I carefully rose to my feet to assess my surroundings. I could see where the pack had played on the bank of the river. Tracks showed chasing, ambushing, and wrestling. This was all practice for the hunt and to establish the hierarchy as the younger wolves developed their endurance and skill, building up to becoming integral members of the pack during pursuit of prey. I saw ungulate bones and small rodents, wild pups' chew toys, still covered in saliva, adorning the meadow. Had I followed the alpha to the rendezvous site? After eight weeks of age, pups are moved from the den to a rendezvous site. Above ground now, the pups learn from their older relatives stalking, pouncing, running, and play mounting (Elbroch and Rinehart 2011). I imagined the pups learning to hunt, seeing where they had dug for ground squirrels, a small mammal their older relatives might view as a trivial food source.

Just downstream of me, I heard a raven call. I moved toward it. Partially submerged in the stream was a freshly killed bull elk. I was already weak from exhaustion and hunger, and the scene in front of me was raw and disturbing. This once majestic being was reduced to sinew and raw meat. I thought of the way packs hunt by running their prey toward the meandering oxbow creeks, singling out the weak or old. The prey has no way to escape but to enter into the water, which slows it down and gives the wolves a better chance of catching it.

I could picture the struggle of the bull elk, and the pack that may have begun feasting even before he released his last breath. Blood was pooled up in the water, the stomach and its contents floating on the surface. I looked down and saw my reflection in the red, muddy water alongside that of the soft white clouds passing overhead. The cavity of the elk had been ripped open. His muzzle faced the sky, his neck twisted, with his antlers submerged under water. Flies had started to accumulate on the carcass and the only sound I could hear now was their incessant buzzing and an occasional call of the raven.

I walked backwards, scanning the area, my heart racing and my body churning with a mixture of adrenaline and fear. I left the carcass and the rendezvous site of the pack and headed toward the meeting location with the rest of the trackers.

I followed the stream to get to the other side of the valley. As I worked my way through the stream stones, I pieced together the wolf pack's story. I imagined that the alpha male had traveled long distances to mark territory and keep a scout watch over the pack. Equally a cornerstone, the alpha female was most likely back at the rendezvous site keeping watch over pups and the rest of the pack. The pack worked with intentional group behavior; the stronger ones provided more for the young and the less skilled hunters. The young were allowed to follow the model the alpha pair set while still participating as integral members of the pack, until it was their time to either step into position as alpha or disperse out on their own.

The wolves would feed on the bull elk for several days before moving on to a new meadow where the elk herd had found temporary solace from the predator. The elk herds moved from meadow to meadow, driven by the pack of wolves and the need for fresh forage untainted by their dung and its accompanying flies. When they moved on to a new feeding ground, they grazed along the edges of the meadow, which kept the forest from encroaching on the grass. As I crossed the stream, I was reminded that this predator-prey relationship is how this land evolved: a constant pulse of disturbance and death resulting in growth and life. Although of course I'd known this in theory, I'd never felt the death aspect of the life cycle so viscerally before. I'd smelled the sweet decay of the forest floor, but the impact of the gutted bull elk was undeniable. The relationship of the wolf and the montane meadow ecosystem resonated deeply with me, and I could not help now but view the land and the earth as a pulsating orb of life and death.

I continued to track and hone my skills in my home state of Washington throughout the year, eagerly awaiting more summers spent with Idaho wilderness wolf packs. I became increasingly aware of the political turmoil developing around wolves. As their populations became successful, with the young dispersing to form new packs, they moved beyond the confines of wilderness areas, and interactions between wolves and livestock became more frequent. Naturally there was a large outcry from both ranchers and defenders of the wolf. I witnessed this firsthand in the summer of 2003.

My friend Nicole and I got lost on a long trek following a pack along Big Creek. Coming across a hunting camp, we approached warily, not sure if we should enter to ask for the best route back toward our camp. The trucks outside the camp had stickers on the bumpers reading "Save an elk, kill a wolf." We kept our lips sealed about our work as we encountered this hostile group of bearded men, who didn't offer to help us. Nicole and I eventually made our way back to camp by sticking to the roads so we could continue to travel late into the night.

The next morning, I set out on a trail of a wolf pack that had been seen near livestock on a private cattle ranch nearby. I found tracks of one individual and began to follow, then suddenly felt my knees get weak. The life that I had sensed in the track felt suddenly extinguished. I was not sure if I should continue to follow the track or not. In the early light of morning I reached out to try to connect again with the track. When I tracked an animal I pictured every detail: its body, the color of its coat, the way it moved its head. I tried to draw up an image of the wolf leaving the tracks that lay before me, but I was having difficulty drawing up the image. Out of nowhere, the experience of my horse accident came back to me. Puzzled, I realized I couldn't connect with the wolf that had left those tracks in the flesh, but

I felt the wolf instead in a timeless land, like where I had gone while my body was lying in the hospital bed.

I continued to follow the track. I could tell it was a female by the tracks' size and shape: slender, less robust than a male's. It was headed in a straight line in the middle of the road. The trail veered into the ditch and over a mountain covered in shale. There, on the craggy hillside with no clear pathway, I lost the trail. It didn't make sense that the wolf would travel that way, in the opposite direction from where I tracked the pack the day before. I knew there was a livestock camp over the mountain along with some cabins, but I did not understand why the wolf veered off the trail instead of continuing along the circuit back toward the pack.

As I trotted back into camp to catch the tail end of breakfast, I heard the news from one of my fellow trackers.

"The alpha female of the pack was shot early this morning when she was attacking calves."

Once again, my knees weakened. When I was out tracking her, I had put myself into the life of that wolf to see what she saw and experience what she experienced. I knew now why the tracks had become lifeless, why I had sensed her in that timeless place. I felt as if part of me was lost too.

As tracking became my way of life and taught me the relationships to nature that I had always desired, it also began to contradict much of how I had learned in school. Nature is not linear. Everything is interconnected and each part plays a role in the larger context of life. Tracking taught me another way of approaching science: holistically.

I read every tracking book and was often able to meet and spend time tracking with the authors of those books. Tracker Louis Liebenberg, author of *The Art of Tracking: The Origin of Science,* described tracking as the oldest science known to humankind. That definition inspired me: Was tracking a pathway to living a life where actions were a conscious act of survival? Was tracking key to understanding how humans can live in harmony with this planet?

I wanted to know how to design my life based on the design of nature, so I drew and studied everything I came across while tracking. I drew every track I could find in detail. I took measurements of each toe and heel pad. I drew each trail, measured how far the next track was from it, and then estimated the width of the animal by calculating the distance between its left to right tracks. I drew the surroundings and the map of the place as it related to the animal's gait. I asked a lot of questions and then immersed myself into exhaustive research in order to answer them. I asked my fellow students and mentors to share their knowledge, too. I read any book I could get my hands on, often visiting libraries to find field guides and books on animal behavior. Then I tracked, usually learning the most through direct observation. Every time I went tracking, I returned with even more questions to delve into.

Once the awareness of patterns in the landscape is turned on, it can't be turned off. This type of observation gives what was once drab and uninteresting or simply scenic a magical beauty. No matter where I went there was always a thirst for curiosity to quench or an adventure to be had.

From the age of sixteen to twenty-four I traveled with the Wilderness Awareness School to Alaska, Canada, Minnesota, and Idaho to track wolves and lead people on expeditions to learn directly from these packs, as well as to assist scientists who were working to preserve these species. The work was meaningful; we brought people out on these expeditions to discover what it meant to be a human in the most basic sense—an animal living on earth.

In 2004 I had the opportunity to travel to Germany, and I was elated to hear of the possibility of tracking some of the first wolves to return to that country from the wilds of Poland. Humans massacred the wolves in Germany in the early twentieth century and into the mid-1960s in Poland. Despite centuries of being aggressively hunted, the packs were beginning to make a comeback, traveling across artificial human borders as their population naturally grew to fill the open space. However, many Europeans still had not forgotten their deeply held hatred of this untamed creature.

October 4, 2004

Spreewitz, Germany

Last night I drove from the castle, where I taught a bird language workshop, to East Germany where the wolves are. Spreewitz is the little village close to the river where three biologists, Sebastian, Gesa, and Elka, live. This is the territory of the only known wolf pack in Germany. There are two adults, three subadults, and five of last year's pups in one pack. It is still unknown if they have had pups this past year. There is a female holding an adjacent territory who has been seen traveling with a male wolf but has not yet had pups.

It is very interesting hearing what these three biologists have been going through to protect these wolves that have returned to Germany. There is a long-standing custom of hatred towards the wolves here and their presence in this village is not welcomed by most.

This morning I had another long breakfast: bread, jellies, cheese, and sausage. The Germans like to linger at the table chatting, which is so different from back home, where it seems like everyone is in a hurry during mealtimes to shovel food down and then get on to the next thing.

Heading out tracking with the biologists, we drove through small villages and neighborhoods to get to the edge of a military training ground where the wolves' core territory is. We drove on back roads to get to where Elka has seen the tracks of the larger male. As soon as we got out of the diesel SUV, we saw fresh tracks of a female wolf. This was so exciting for me, to be on the trail of the wolf again. I followed her for a long way as she trotted into an opening. The opening was surrounded by dense pine forest, covered in needles and the occasional mushroom. It was a desolate region stripped for mining. As the wolf got into the opening she walked in an overstep walk, her hind foot landing ahead of her front in the track pattern. She was out of her baseline gait of a trot, most likely slowing to assess the area for danger from humans, traveling slow, looking around. Tracks of deer, wild swine, red fox, and badger all crossed her trail. This was the first time since I arrived in Germany that I saw these tracks so clear in sand. I could see every detail of the tracks I had been having a difficult time deciphering in the forest debris in other parts of the country. The deer here are so small! Their tracks look like our fawn tracks back home.

I wanted to trail the female wolf from the point where she was last seen, but Gesa wanted to find the tracks of the male and see if the two were traveling together. We continued down a large sandy road toward a massive coal mine looming in the distance. As we traveled we crossed over many trails of the deer, swine, and elk. The red fox was traveling along the road as those trails crossed.

We picked up old tracks of the male wolf and followed. We found the place where Elka was with her dog Jack yesterday. We found fresh tracks of the female wolf from last night going to investigate Jack's tracks. She left a scat on the heather bush, a signal to Jack, and then went back and continued her route. I watched as the dung beetles busily took bits of the scat and rolled them over to holes to bury them. The balls they were rolling were as big as or bigger than the beetles themselves. We found several areas where the dung beetles had buried scat and we also found several beetle carcasses along the multi-species wildlife trails.

After Gesa collected the wolf scat from the female wolf in a plastic bag, we continued to follow her tracks. She went up a ridge and cut off to follow a trail along the ridge. As we followed her tracks along the ridge, where the wolf could look out onto the large expanse of sand edged with pine forests, we found what we were looking for: fresh tracks of the male wolf. They were traveling together. This is exactly what Gesa wanted to see. The female wolf birthed nine hybrid pups last year that had to be killed in order to maintain the genetic integrity of wolves. Wolves breeding with domestic dogs could mean trouble for the farmers. A hybrid has wild instincts from the wolf yet, from the domestic side, is not afraid of humans, so may attack livestock more frequently. Better to keep the wolves wild and away from humans as much as possible. The wolf was fitted with a radio collar so the biologists could keep a close watch to make sure she was not still interested in domestic dogs. The hope is that she will breed with this wolf this coming season.

Sebastian, Gesa, and Elka told me of the political, social, and economic complications they needed to deal with. East Germany is similar to the places I track in Idaho, except this is the land where the fear and hatred of wolves originated. As we drove around through towns, I noticed statues of wolves and asked Gesa what they were. She explained they were erected where the last of the wolves in that area were killed, as a celebration of sorts. Gesa looks forward to the day when the wolves repopulate those areas and they find the scats of the wolves at the base of those statues.

Across the globe, the interplay of human against predator has played out to the extreme. Stories such as Little Red Riding Hood, told to young children, have instilled an exaggerated fear of wolves for centuries. Predator myths have been propagated to fill the gaps of the unknown. Fear of the unknown can only be alleviated by the deliberate act of connection.

I've seen this pattern the world over, from my encounters in Idaho and Germany to my experiences much later when I traveled with my husband to Botswana to track the endangered African painted dogs. We don't tend to what we fear, and as we become divorced from nature, we fear those wild predators who, it turns out, keep the world in balance. When will we learn that wild animals need wilderness, and, crucially, vice versa?

It was not a coincidence that I found myself in the presence of packs of canids around the globe, learning their interdependency to place, learning the vital role of death in life. But neither was it something I had dreamed of since I was a child. It was simply where I naturally arrived when I took the time to ask: *What is this earth where I live? How can I interact and be part of nature? What should I do with my life?* I sent these questions to a place as mysterious as creation itself, perhaps to the place I'd glimpsed after my horse accident. I asked in reverence and in awe of the grace I experienced when I let myself be immersed in the natural order. I trusted the answers I received from the earth like the wolf must trust her pack.

Three things we can all learn from wolves

Nomadic hunter-gathers were the first to see the connection humans had with wolves. The grey wolf *Canis lupus* was the first animal to be domesticated by humans in a mutual relationship, sharing food and living amongst each other. That bond felt with your pet dog is an ancient friendship.

PACK DYNAMICS

One of the most immediate lessons you can learn from wolves is how essential the group dynamics are. The alpha male and female share leadership equally, and their role as leaders is not to boss the pack around and lie back while everyone else does the work; alpha wolves spend every second making sure their pack is strong, fed, and safe. Pups are not isolated from the pack to do "kid stuff"; rather they spend their time playing near the adults, emulating the adult wolves and learning from them how to be a wolf. Wolves put the health of their pack before everything else, always protecting their weakest. We can learn from wolves that it is not the strength of the individual that matters, but rather the strength of the whole, and the pack is only as strong as the weakest link. It is the role of the alpha pair to make sure that health and vitality is present in every member of the pack. We learn leadership from the alpha pair because if those leaders are not strong, if they are not leading by example and working hard, the whole pack begins to break down.

PREDATOR AND PREY

The predator-prey relationship is how life on our planet evolved: a constant pulse of disturbance and death resulting in growth and life. I learned in the wilderness while tracking wolves that prey rely on predators just as much as predators rely on prey. The wolves while hunting tend to single out the weak prey, therefore keeping the whole prey herd stronger by removing the weakest or the sick. We tend to use the predator-prey relationship as a metaphor for who is weak (the prey) and who is strong (the predator). But wolves, an archetypal predator, are fully reliant on the health of the "weak" populations they feed on. So who is really weak, and who is strong? What is the true relationship between predator and prey? This is the lesson I have built my life around: we humans, who see ourselves as invincible, are in fact fully dependent on the health of the planet that feeds us, and just because we feed from something doesn't make us superior. In fact, it makes us utterly dependent.

KEEP MOVING

Wolves spend 28 to 50 percent of their lives traveling. They are the ultimate athlete, able to swim in flowing rivers, sustain a fast run for 20 minutes at a time, and can cover up to 45 miles in a single night. But their movement isn't for movement's sake, and they always find the path of least resistance through the terrain they traverse. They work hard and intelligently. It is within this movement that more life is produced. We learn that even plants rely on predators, because of something called the trophic cascade. The predators keep the herd of prey moving, which in turn allows the plants to regrow and be more available to the other forms of life like the beavers and songbirds. Really there is nothing in nature that is able to be truly sedentary. Wolves move for their food, and in turn that moves their food. The herds of elk move and that in turn moves the plants. The plants are allowed to grow more and collect energy from the sun. That sun energy then moves into the soil and sequesters carbon. We have seen the results of movement of herds on our own ranch, where by mimicking the wolves and elk with humans and cattle we are seeing more biodiversity in plant life and more carbon is being sequestered in the soil. It is within the lessons from the wolf that I have found the solution to tending to grasslands and herds of cattle. We keep them moving, and in turn that brings more life.

Vision

Spiritual questions had been growing alongside my nature connection from the beginning of my time at Wilderness Awareness School. I understood that as much as I was tracking through the wilderness, I was seeking out vision through inner-tracking.

While at WAS, the earth had provided a place for me to learn to value my body and the connection of my body to my mind and spirit—it was impossible to track well if those three parts of myself weren't in harmony. I overcame my insecurities after being violated. I learned earth skills as a humble student, understanding that I was small in proportion to the vastness of creation. I could build a debris hut, trap animals, build fires, forage for edible plants, and track wildlife. I saw most people in our culture measured their worth by mastering a subject, dedicating their lives to conquering a mountain, exploiting forests for profit, or building bigger, stronger houses in which to live. I did not understand how people could mentally separate themselves from stewarding the land and people in favor of accumulating material wealth. The human-made environment was at odds with the wilderness. The regenerative life in nature was the true designer of functional living systems, continuously creating more life. As a human, I was also nature and I too wanted my actions to regenerate life.

During my teenage years at Wilderness Awareness School, I was seeking a rite of passage from youth to adulthood. I was not interested in the compartmentalized and shallow approach to a rite of passage: getting a driver's license when I turned sixteen, going to prom, or graduating. When I was immersed in nature I felt that my body was merely a collection of molecules joined with the particles of the soil and all living things, no separation. From this place of no separation with nature, I sought my vision.

At seventeen years old, after I had been immersed in the wilderness for two and a half years, traveled to Alaska and Idaho to track wolves, tested my skills against ninjas, and spent countless hours at my secret spot, I walked out my front door to sit on the porch. I watched a red-tailed hawk preening herself as she perched on a bigleaf maple tree. It was a leisurely morning and I had nothing to do but sit on the porch, run my fingers through my hair, and ponder the small drops of rain that fell on the wet grass. For the hawk that was every day, except for the occasional hunt or caring for young. Even the hunt and the harshness of nature were tangibly justified, creating an oscillation of life and death.

Rocking back and forth in the creaking chair, I was facing a juncture in my personal trail. Struggling with choices and projecting the path ahead was creating an inner turmoil. Should I go back to school to pursue a degree that could potentially support my desires to live close to nature? I had been paving my own way since I fell off Sundance at thirteen years old and had been the character in the play of my own choices. Now, at age seventeen, I was stuck. As I sat, I pondered that the tree always knew which way to grow and the ant had a path to follow. The ant would simply travel around any obstruction and end up right back on the same path, never stuck. But I lacked vision of a comprehensible future. I didn't know then that tracking was, fittingly, the path that would carry me into my future.

Wearing jeans and a T-shirt with a small foldup knife in my pocket, I decided to head to Linne Doran, the place where I knew the woods the best after exploring it nearly every day for over two years. Hoping not to run in to anyone, I parked my car, got out, and began my walk. Dark clouds were moving in, the air was crisp, and the inside of my nose was tingling when I breathed in. I was wearing sandals and I already felt a chill.

I came to Anne's Airstream on the edge of the woods owned by Weyerhaeuser, an international timber company. Beyond those woods was the expanse of National Forest lands in the Cascade Mountains. I felt comfortable there. I would often sleep out for days in huts that I made from branches, ferns, debris from the forest floor, and cattails.

Opening the door of the Airstream, I was pleasantly surprised to find a pair of warm boots just inside the door. I
set my sandals down in the place of the boots. I knew Anne
would not mind me borrowing them. She was always looking
out for me.

Continuing my walk down the dirt road, I passed by the
Inipi, or sweatlodge, site and paused before continuing on.
There were two Inipis built from willow saplings stuck into
the ground and bent to form a round hut. A large fire pit lay
in the middle and small altars made of mounded-up dirt with
small rocks to form a circle marked the opening of the two
lodges. The altars could not be made of just any dirt; only
dirt that had been pushed up by a mole. This mole-dirt altar
represented the earth. Each week I spent a day preparing those
lodges, gathering and splitting firewood, raking the grounds,
and covering the lodges with thick blankets to keep any light
from entering inside during the ceremony.

In preparation for the ceremony, rocks the size of a bowl-
ing ball would be placed in a circle in the fire pit, starting in
the west, moving to the north, east, and then south, followed
by one signifying the earth and one the sky. After the first six
were set just right, more rocks were piled on those and then
a fire would be lit to burn hot for many hours until red coals
covered the stones in a heaping mound.

Pausing to check the site for cleanliness, I was reminded of
the prayers I had been reciting every day. Praying for the spirit
powers always came first. Then came all creation. I prayed for

rejuvenation of the plants and animals, that they may flourish
in balance on this earth. I prayed that the waters would run
clean and the fish would return to the streams. I prayed for
the people, those I held close in my heart as well as those who
were struggling. Lastly, I prayed for myself, that I would find
a path in my life that would be helpful for the earth for many
generations into the future.

My adoptive Lakota father, Gilbert Tatanka Mani, meaning
Walking Bull, taught me how to pray in this sequence, what
he called "an orderly fashion." He had arrived at our school
one day in 1996, the same year I began with WAS, carrying
a duffle bag filled with a change of clothes and sacred items.
He never made plans about where to go next; he just always
seemed to be at the right place at the right time. Gilbert was
born in the summer of 1930 in a teepee in the Black Hills
outside the town of Hot Springs, South Dakota. He didn't attend missionary schools as a youth, but instead was raised with
his own Lakota language and tradition in a camp near Wan-
blee, South Dakota. Traditional knowledge intact, he was guided by the spirits throughout his life, and one day those spirits
guided him to our little school in the woods, so he would
say. His small house was set up right next to the Inipi. People
would visit him there and he would conduct ceremony in a
sacred way. He said prayers to bring abundance of salmon back
to the rivers and streams, thick berries back to the bushes,
and healthy grasses for the deer and elk. The first fall after he
set up the ceremonial grounds, the salmon came back to the

streams, which had not seen the fish in years. The following spring, the bushes around the Inipi were thick with berries.

Gilbert had taken me under his wing, recognizing that I was without a father in this world. He called me *Maka-Win*, or Earth Woman, and recognized that I was set on living a life in accordance with the principles he was sharing with us. He was teaching me his songs, ceremonies, and traditions. I would sit and listen to Gilbert's stories next to the ceremony grounds where he was often found. He spoke to the birds and they would surround him. He was like St. Francis of Assisi in the stories my grandmother used to tell me, birds gathered around him as he praised all of creation. Gilbert never had children of his own, and in a ceremonial way he adopted me as his daughter.

I'd spent many hours here with him, and now an overwhelming feeling of comfort and confidence came over me as I stood at those sacred grounds of prayer. I walked with an extra perk in my step while the darkness of the second-growth Douglas fir and hemlock trees engulfed me. Picking up on a deer trail, I was drawn to follow the track. I felt again that way of being in peace at my secret spot when I reached out to touch the doe. Starting in the dark and damp forest, the tracks guided me out to an area that had been logged recently, the slash still covering the ground, making it difficult to travel. My legs lifted high, up over the fallen logs and blackberries that had lost their leaves, but the sharp thorns persisted on the stalks, grabbing me every few steps. As I trailed the deer, I started to notice how my own body was following in the movement of the animal, internalized by now from the countless hours of following deer trails. I felt myself moving effortlessly as I glanced down and saw an indent in the ground about every one and a half feet, where the pointed tracks set down after the legs lifted up over sticks, brambles, and logs. Out of the corner of my eye I saw woody browse on a maple tree still wet with saliva. This trail was fresh.

In the distance I could see a clearing, and I was grateful that I would be getting out of the tangle of blackberries reaching out to catch my hair and snag my clothes. As I approached this clearing, a smell wafted over me—it was the worst stench I could imagine, one that could only be from humans, like a man's dirty sock basket. Covering my nose, I continued into a vast sea of muck. The deer had worn the trail through this substance until the side of the trail was up to my thighs. It was light green and pulverized, like the clippings from a lawn mower, smelling so foreign compared to the surrounding forests of sweet hemlock and fir needles. It was a chemical smell with an anaerobic steam lifting off of it like smoke. In the distance stood the doe that I had been tracking. Something was different about her. Nearly half of her hair had fallen out. She was sick, most likely from eating the substance, which smelled of chemical-laden green waste.

Hastily continuing through the muck, I found the tire tracks of dump trucks that had worn a large area for continual dumping. The tracks of the trucks were interrupting the travel

route of the deer. It was like the drivers had chosen this spot
because they thought no one would be looking; the road was
overgrown and abandoned. That doe may have followed this
trail her whole life, starting out as a fawn trailing her mother.
Most likely, many generations of deer had also followed the
same path before her. There were many trails that came from
the woods and led to the opening. The dumpsite had previously been a grassy meadow where the deer would come to
graze. A deep sadness came over me. I did not want to leave
the wilderness and that doe. I wanted to protect her. She was
being mistreated by humans oblivious or callous to the ruin-
ation they were creating.

Walking along the logging road, I started to regain my ori-
entation. I was close to a spot we WAS students called Cedar
Falls. A large cedar tree had tumbled over the waterfall and
was wedged in the pool below. I had climbed up from the base
of the tree to the top of the waterfall many times, lying there
in exhilaration at being so close to the powerful waterfall as
white water cascaded off the cliff.

The storm clouds were building and a wet snow began to
fall. Watching as the flakes landed on the road in front of me,
dissipating into water as they touched the land, I knew I had
to find a spot for the night and begin building a shelter. It was
a long way back to my car, and I felt a pull in my heart to stay
despite the snow. A small trail led off the main logging road
downstream of Cedar Falls. On the lookout for a decent shelter
for the night, I paused along the trail by a large hollowed-out

cedar stump lying on its side. I considered stuffing it with debris to fill all the air space, mimicking a squirrel nest where I could wriggle inside to stay warm. I assessed my surroundings. I could pack moss in the cracks of the log that were exposed to the falling snow. A few fallen fir trees in the surroundings would yield bark to keep the snow out of the openings at either end of the stump. I could cut some vine maple branches and make a large wreath to stuff sword fern, hemlock branches, and cedar boughs to form a thick plug to wedge in the entrance after I made my way in for the night. I calculated that all of this work would take me about three hours and I would get intermittent sleep in that dark, damp cave. I could do the work before darkness set in.

But I hesitated. I did not have fond memories of the last hollowed cedar stump I slept in along the Skykomish River, when the nightmare had seized me and I'd ended up without shelter because of it. I did not want my night at Cedar Falls to be like that frightening night. I continued down the trail toward the falls, abandoning the idea of staying in the stump. But the snow had started to fall in larger flakes, my hair and clothes were wet, and if I paused I felt the cold take over my body; I needed shelter soon. Approaching the stream I found a large standing cedar tree that had a hollow in the base of its trunk. The cedar, also known as *arborvitae*, meaning tree of life, was historically used for houses by the Pacific Northwest Indigenous tribes (Stewart 1984).

The snow was no longer melting now, and the flakes were

tucking into just the right spots to blanket the earth. But under the tree it was dry and the lower branches hung dead, protected by the boughs above. Reaching up, I broke off one of the dry dead branches hanging from the cedar tree. I pulled out my pocketknife and started carving a spindle. It was about five inches long and one inch in diameter. I carved off the bark, smoothed the outside, and made a slight point on each end. I then carved a flat fireboard about an inch thick out of a larger dead branch of the same tree. I pulled out a lace from the boots I was wearing and took a section of the branch that had a slight curve in it to make a bow, then attached the string to the bow. Along the stream I found a rock with a depression in it that fit nicely in the palm of my hand. I used that as a handhold for the top of the spindle. With the string of the bow wrapped around the spindle, I set one end of the spindle on the fireboard and the stone on top of the upright spindle. I pressed firmly with my left hand on top of the stone. I braced my wrist against the front of my leg, just above my ankle, wrapping my arm around my leg. With my right hand I moved the bow back and forth in a sawing motion with smooth, even strokes.

I had practiced bowdrill for countless hours until my hands bled from blisters. At WAS we all challenged ourselves by gathering wet hardwood in the pouring rain. A bowdrill spindle should be made of soft, dry, non-resinous wood; however, we were always looking for ways to challenge each other so that when it really mattered the most we had survival skills we could rely on. That night in the snow I was hoping all my practice would get me through to the morning.

I bowed now back and forth. Faster and faster I drilled, spinning the spindle. As the dust built up in the notch I had carved in the fire board, the smoke rose up from where the spindle met the board. The dark dust from the fire was so thick now it spread out on top of the board. As I slowed the spinning down, I carefully lifted the spindle from the board, making sure not to knock the dust out of the pie-shaped notch. I peered down close to see if a red ember had formed. As the smoke dissipated and the kinetic friction stopped, what lay before me was a pile of blackish wood dust with no ember.

Before the board and spindle had a chance to completely cool in the air, I went at it again, bowing back and forth. Starting a fire was the only way I could stay warm. I needed to use the hollowed arch of the tree as a reflector and a shelter from the snow. The smoke started billowing at the base of the spindle. I went faster and the smoke rose up all around the spindle. I was pretty sure I had heated up the dust enough for it to form a coal, but I wanted to be sure, so I gave it a few more fast strokes, pushing down with my weight on the stone. As I pushed, the spindle popped out of the fireboard and the dust went flying.

My bowdrill kit was now strewn out in front of me. All the warmth I'd built up dispersed, and I collapsed in exhaustion. I considered walking back to my car, but I knew it was too late. It would be too dangerous to travel at night. The darkness was fast approaching, and I could easily get disoriented and lost. I was committed.

Mustering up the dregs of my energy, I put the pieces of my fire kit back together and began a slow, steady rhythmic sawing motion. I quieted my mind and focused on the wood dust emerging into the V-shaped notch. As I took deep, concentrated breaths, the smoke slowly started to rise. I pictured the ember forming. I paced myself, making sure I was building the heat and the wood dust simultaneously. The dust had to get to eight hundred degrees before it would ignite. Body shaking and wet with sweat, I spun the spindle. The smoke was so thick now. I careened my head over to the side, not wanting to stop for fear of losing the heat. I entered into a thoughtless trance like I had when I was running after the white wolf in Alaska. I saw the smoke coming not just from the friction of wood on wood, but from below the dust in the notch. Slowly I lifted the spindle off of the board and set it, the bow, and the rock handhold to the side. I got down eye level with the fireboard and peered into the dust. A red ember glowed. I had made a coal!

The precious coal from a friction fire is as fragile as a newborn baby. I gently reached down and lifted the fireboard away from the coal, which was resting on a leaf I had placed below the notch in the board. Lifting the leaf slowly, I poured the ember and dust into a nest of loosened red cedar bark and the driest, finest twigs I could find. I slowly blew the coal until the bundle I held ignited. I set the flame in the wood structure

I had built from the dead hanging branches of the cedar tree and other hemlock trees nearby. I'd placed the wood in a teepee shape, with the smallest, toothpick-sized sticks in the center, gradually getting larger as the teepee went outward. I placed the flaming nest of bark and wood inside the opening of the stick teepee, made to look like a door. Flames engulfed the structure.

Collapsed with my back up against the hollowed-out cedar trunk, I gazed out at the large snowflakes falling like white gems from the sky. This was the first time I had actually depended on a fire for my survival rather than just for my comfort. With a storm brewing and the chill from my wet clothes beginning to absorb into my body, the fire saved me. I had my place for the night. With the fire lit, warmth and sleep would follow.

I gathered more wood to get me through the night. I also gathered bark to set up as a heat reflector, and to pull over me when I took my wet clothes off to keep drafts from chilling my naked skin. Walking past the stream at the base of the waterfall, I paused to look into the clear water. Reflected back at me were smooth pebbles of browns and greys. I remembered a story that a Haida wood carver, Ralph Bennett, once told me of his people, who lived in the Pacific Northwest. The story recounts a time when the rivers were so thick with salmon that you could walk across their backs to cross the river and never touch the stones below. I imagined salmon so thick in the streams you could just reach down and throw one up on the bank, feasting on the richness they had brought from the ocean to the fresh waters.

Back at my fire, I said the prayers Gilbert had taught me. I prepared for sleep that night warm in the womb of the grandmother cedar tree, knowing I could live here forever, surviving on food I gathered and staying warm with the shelters and fires I built. I could build traps for squirrels and rabbits. I could find cattail swamps and dig up the roots, extracting the starch and feasting on the young shoots that emerge early in the spring. I could make jerky, tan hides for clothes, and make a bow and arrow for hunting. The possibilities were endless. I stoked the fire until I was warm enough to fall asleep, peaceful in the knowledge I had the skills to survive here as long as I needed.

That night I was in and out of a dream state. I awoke shivering. The fire had died down, so once more I stoked it. My clothes hung propped up on sticks around the fire to dry. I went to sleep again, dreaming of the salmon coming back to the rivers and of the wolf packs that once flourished in this wilderness. Waking up tired, I stoked the fire hot and fell into a deep sleep.

I awoke a final time to the faint light of dawn. A foul smell had shaken me out of my dream state. It wasn't the smell of the gunk that was causing deer to lose their hair and a meadow ecosystem to perish. This was the smell of…burning clothes. My clothes had caught on fire! I jolted up, looking at the fragments of Carhartt jeans. The waist had survived, but the legs were burnt up to the seam. My shirt too was a fragment of thread, useless for anything but wiping up a mess. I was naked and alone in the wilderness, far from any road or house and surrounded by a blanket of snow.

I put the remains of my fire out, that fire that I'd worked so hard for and that had taken it upon itself to teach me a lesson. It had taken away the possessions I'd brought with me, rendering me as helpless as the deer in the poisoned meadow. The lesson showed me the struggle to survive in the wilderness was a struggle that humans have brought upon themselves by going away from the natural patterns and law of the earth. We have forgotten not only how to survive, but also how to caretake the elements necessary for our survival.

During my time alone at Cedar Falls, I heard the creatures crying out to me for help. The salmon wanted the obstructions to be cleared so they could run again in great numbers. The deer wanted their forests to be lush again so they could thrive on the purity of plants. The waters cried out to flow clean of chemicals and sediment that ran off from the clear-cut. The clear-cuts had been sprayed with herbicide to prevent the weedy vegetation from coming back and covering the earth. Those weeds that were being stopped would have rebuilt the soil to allow the natural succession back to forests. I too was stripped of my covering like the forest, and it was now time for me to rebirth.

I walked out of the woods naked. It was a symbolic walk for me as I moved down logging roads and wildlife trails without the need or want of a single material item. I had, after all, long since placed the health of the earth above the want for any material possession. I did not feel defeated; I felt galvanized by this unplanned rite of passage. I needed to leave the wilderness now, but I resolved that I would return to the wild and flourish. I would learn to live in a way that created abundance, instead of merely surviving for my life, living alone in the wilderness, away from my friends and family. I would find a way to love the earth and be part of its regeneration. The fire I had lit with the bowdrill was inside me now, and it would continue to burn throughout my life.

In the months that followed the night at Cedar Falls, I sat up in the Inipi on overnight vision quests to seek out and clarify my path in life. The visions I received would become magnified into an urgent need for action. I sat up all night, asking for a vision in the way Gilbert Walking Bull had instructed me. This type of concentrated meditation into my direction in life created a bloodhound focus on my future.

"Doniga, you need to make a choice. Do not get stuck at a crossroads. We can't just wait around for a messiah to come fix things for us," Gilbert told me after I had emerged from one of my overnight vision quests. He had a gentle but stern way of speaking. The expressions on his face matched the tone of his voice as his dark bushy eyebrows raised up and down to match his pitch. "Each one of us has sacred powers within ourselves to actually get up and *do* something." He accentuated *do* in a low guttural voice that made me jump on the edge of my seat. "If you really work towards things, put your mind, spirit, heart, soul, and body together and then put your feet on a sacred path, you will have the tools to move forward. It is not up to us to sit here in the world, look around and say, 'Hey, the world is going to come to an end and there is no hope.' We were not given the power by the great spirit to see the future like that. We were given the choice as caretakers to move and do something significant in life. You just need to focus on that." Here I was, sitting in the presence of a man who came from a lineage of greatly respected and powerful people: his great-grandfather Sitting Bull, his grandfather a holy man Moves Camp, with other relatives of Horn Chips and Crazy Horse, all legendary Lakotas whose vision shaped the outcome of history.

He went on to tell of his youth to relate to what I was going through. "When I was sixteen or seventeen I had a vision from the Great Spirit. They told me that there is nothing greater than each individual and that nothing is impossible. I was raised around holy men and holy women who had these sacred powers and I have seen miraculous healings. Did you know that, Doniga? Humans need to realize that the people are here to stay and we must be smart about things. When I was a little kid the system was so strong and powerful in our little camp because we kept our tradition alive, yet as I got older it broke down. The system I am talking about is our Lakota way of life. I was taught from a young age to respect nature as sacred. But I saw other Lakotas around me go away from nature and our sacred ways. We need to respect all things in nature. This is not being practiced the way it was when I was a young child."

He told me of the stories from his youth when he was sent to live with his grandparents who were amongst a group of holy people living in a small village and continuing their original ways. Instead of being forced into missionary schools, he was sent to be trained by his grandparents in Lakota ceremonial ways. They had to do so in secret; at that time it was illegal for them to practice their ceremonies.

"There will be no wars anymore if people see the sacred powers in the animals and that they are supporting us in a way. We need to pray to them and in turn they will help us. Help us to build something between all races. We can heal people mentally. That is what this is all about if we recognize it."

When Gilbert put it that way, I really listened, hung onto every word like an integral piece to a larger puzzle. It was about positive manifestation. Prayer equal to work. I vowed to never work just for money; I decided that all the work I did in life would be a prayer, put toward a greater purpose. Gilbert taught me that I must learn to use my mind and thoughts carefully to cultivate power, not be scattered all over the place. When he was growing up there were values that each child was taught and expected to follow, which he then taught me so that one day I could teach my own children.

One sunny afternoon shortly after a vision quest, Gilbert and I were sitting outside the Inipi on logs that were yet to be split. We would often sit and I would ask questions or he would just be inspired to tell me a story or teach me a song. This day I could tell he had a particular lesson he would teach me. "This is all we have in life to separate good from evil," he would explain. "Children are born pure. Once they develop thought, they need to have role models and values to live by." That day he taught me the values and principles of how to achieve the upright mind. He explained to me *Wo-ope Sa-Kowin*: seven sacred principles of the Lakota people. I took these on in my life, using them as a guidepost that I would later teach to my own children.

The first, *Wo-wa-h'wa ka,* he explained to me, is the inner quietness that every human possesses when they calm their mind and feel at peace with themselves and their surroundings. That was it! That is how the deer finally accepted me at my secret spot. It took me months to get a glimpse into this practice, but I was able to achieve it. Sensory absorption and letting thoughts drift away was the key to unlocking this principle! It was something that was only achieved when everyday worries became released and the quietness and tranquility emerged out of connection with senses. It took spending time alone in nature with a quiet mind for long periods of time. It is a way of sensing intently as though everything is new, not a judgment based on past experiences or worries about the future.

I sat there listening to Gilbert speak under the clear sky, with the smell of a fire nearby. I practiced *Wo-wa-h'wa ka*, taking everything in. I noticed that when I was tuned in to not just the words that were being said but the other senses I was experiencing, I internalized it. It was a crisp day, and the buds of the elderberry shrubs were a vibrant green all wrapped up from the cold, ready to burst open as soon as the warming air engulfed them. A song sparrow fed on the ground nearby. Gilbert had a way of drawing people in when he spoke. Often his voice would go to a whisper so that I had to listen intently. When he spoke he didn't always form what we call complete sentences, but concepts came through more clearly than when others spoke. It was the way of his native language to speak in images instead of being concerned about the order of words.

The second sacred principle is *Wo-cante' k*na-ke*. This, he explained, is to have love and compassion for those close to you. *Cante'* means heart or within your heart. *K*nake* is those that you place in. Gilbert instructed me to ask the Great Spirit to bless those that I keep in my heart. These included my relatives, friends, and people who needed help. It was easy to do for my family; I knew that no matter what happened we would always be there for each other. But I thought about all the people I had come across in my journeys. I had lost trust in so many people for what they had done to disgrace the earth and its people, like prioritizing their own accumulation of wealth over the future of the planet. I had to somehow reach inside to have compassion for those people.

The third principle he taught me was *Wo-wa unsi-la*. He explained that it is similar to *Wo-cante' k*na-ke*, but it is extended out to all of creation. It is the deep caring for all living things, including the animals, the roots, the trees, and all of nature. This principle was much easier for me to internalize than the previous one. I cared so much about the animals, the plants, and the trees. At that point in my life I would go out and talk to the trees and they would listen, and sometimes I would go out and listen to the trees and they would talk to me.

Gilbert told me a story about his grandmother. She was a medicine woman. When he was a young child, she would send him out to gather the medicine in the form of plants and roots. She would send him long distances and create a detailed verbal map for him. She said he needed to travel far to one specific area to gather a medicine plant for her. When he set out on his journey, he walked past several of the plants she wanted him to gather. He would never think to just get the easy one for his grandmother, because she was looking for a plant that grew in one specific place. This place, she had told him, was over a hill that was shaped like the back of a buffalo. It was alongside a stream to the north of where the two streams came together. As he would go out on these walks alone he would notice things. He would notice the anthills and how the ants all worked together to build their mounds and gather food. He would notice the deer that grazed along the creek banks. In this way he developed a deep respect for all of creation. He developed a compassion for all living things and a caring for all people just as the medicine that his grandmother had him gather healed people. He witnessed this healing when people came from all over the country to his village. They came to see his grandparents, who were healers. His family did not judge anyone who came for healing. It did not matter the color of their skin or where they came from. If they were open and asking for help, his people would help them. It was a selfless service to others and to all creation.

The healing that took place in his village came from their following the fourth principle. *Wo-wa-wo-ki-ye*, he explained, is to take your feelings and use them to help those in need. This principle of making yourself useful and taking action is what causes people to reach out to those in need and help them. It can be displayed in acts such as cutting firewood for an elderly neighbor or bringing food to a family that has just had a baby.

"When I was a young boy, it was my job to ride my horse up in the hills where the elderlies lived." Gilbert referred to his elders as "elderlies" in an affectionate way. "I had a good time riding my horse up in the hills, checking on them to see if they needed water or firewood. If they needed wood, the other young boys and I would go down to the water and drag limbs up for their fire, or we would carry water for them. In my lifetime it felt good helping the elderlies." It is not enough to feel the grief or sorrow that others held; you have to do something about it.

As I sat listening to Gilbert I knew that my next step was to take the visions I had received from my quests and put them into action. I needed to nourish people and nourish the earth at the same time.

Wo-bli-he-cha, the fifth sacred principle, is the feeling of being fully alive, enjoying each and every moment of life. He explained to me it is that feeling when you jump into cold water and the only thing you can experience is that exhilarating moment when your entire body tingles with aliveness. It is not until all the first four principles are achieved that you will achieve this fifth principle, he explained. I recognized that my inner turmoil throughout my teenage years, such as when I felt trapped in school, or when I was running away from home and rebelling against my mother, could be expressed as a lack of *Wo-bli-he-cha*. I hadn't been able to achieve that feeling when I wasn't in the wild. It was in the wilderness I felt fully alive, where I felt like I was living the potential of being human. I had not yet been able to achieve this feeling when I was not in the wild.

The sixth principle is *Wo-wi-yu-ski*. This is an overwhelming, heartfelt joy that comes from the childlike curiosity, wonder, and delight in each moment or in each aspect of creation that is encountered. It is the positive power that keeps people active and industrious in life. Gilbert was no stranger to hard work. At that time in his late sixties he would split and haul firewood and outwork all of us teenagers, and have a smile on his face the entire time. He made the most menial task have joy and wonder, like a child running for the first time.

The seventh principle is *Wi-co-za-ni*, the sacred state of health of mind, body, and spirit. It is only when the previous six principles are practiced that one can achieve *Wi-co-za-ni*. It is the instinctual powers that come about when the connection of mind, body, and spirit are all working together. Gilbert had me imagine the quickness of a wolf living in the moment without mundane thoughts bogging it down. He explained that this principle was displayed in those who are alert and aware. His great-uncle Crazy Horse was the epitome of *Wi-co-za-ni* for his people, in the way he evaded the bullet in battle with instinctive agility and sacred medicine.

"Today is a new day. Treat it like it is the beginning of time and you can cause your body to be in a constant state of health as long as you activate these powers within your brain and conduct yourself according to these seven sacred principles," he told me as we sat breathing in the cold air. "This is the key to longevity, health, and happiness. Every day is a sacred event and it must be your choice when you wake up in the morning to live by these principles and keep your mind upright. This is what will heal the world of troubles." He emphasized *choice* and looked me straight in the eye when he said the word. It was meant for me. I needed to choose in life what would transcend the materialistic and bring the earth, people, and myself a hope for the future by living a meaningful life.

I felt that day that I had obtained the secret of life. I wasn't living by these principles when I was running away into the wilderness, planning never to return. I wasn't living by them when I left my mother a note on my bed, knowing that her heart would ache in my absence. I wasn't living by them when I was eaten up with loathing of humans' greed, when I hated them for poisoning meadows, for clear-cutting forests. The lack of this system of care, these principles, had left me flailing many times, seeking something without a true moral compass. Understanding these principles gave my life a greater purpose: I was a caretaker of the earth and all creation.

I no longer looked grimly upon the flawed design of the built environment. I knew a built environment could be a beautiful, intentional, useful, and beneficial thing. Observing a squirrel build a nest, and witnessing the lush life in the wetlands created when the beaver built its dam, proved to me that all creatures can have a positive impact on the earth, and I now believed that this was true of humans too. I would study and apply the masterful chaos and design of nature to my life and the lives of others. I vowed to find ways to learn from my experience of surviving in the fractured wilderness and apply them to thriving into bountiful permanence. I would provide not only for my family and myself, but for all people. I would find a way to give forward all that I had learned. This is what I vowed as I sat there listening to Gilbert speak of his ways.

I had to take my experiences of tracking and observing patterns in nature beyond passive observations, though. So far I had done my best not to leave a trace on the ecosystem, but

I knew I needed to use the principles Gilbert had taught me and take a more active and intentional role.

In previous years as a vagabond I ate from the waste thrown away in dumpsters by people in the towns across the west. I kept a portion, albeit a small one, of the 40 percent of food wasted in the United States from ending up in the landfill and releasing methane that warms our oceans (Gunders 2012), and felt proud of that. But most of that food was empty nutrition, grown in soil lacking in the previously intact microbiology, which had been present before the fields were plowed and poisoned. It was the opposite of the food I had since found in the wilderness, where the species were dense with nutrients and not hampered genetically by humans.

I entered into the wilderness to survive upon resources that had been slashed, poisoned, and extracted for profit. Even in that precarious wilderness, the food available to me was incredibly nutrient dense, far more so than the abundant food I'd found in dumpsters. One day of sipping wild ginger tea while eating a handful of fresh cattail shoots placed on sticks over a fire to grill after a foraging walk on huckleberries, salmonberries, stinging nettles, and miner's lettuce brought me more vital nutrients than months of supermarket food grown in a monoculture.

Learning how to insulate my shelter from the squirrel and tend to my family and food source like the wolf brought me to a vision of agriculture with permanence. This vision of agriculture was to mimic the historical ideal I held so strong in my mind, when the band-tailed pigeons flew in such great numbers that they shut out the sun like a cloud, and when, by the thousands, they landed on a tree and the birds would take up every space on each branch (Anderson 2005). Humans could design agriculture systems to mimic the birds to serve the function of adding fertility across the landscape like the band-tailed pigeons of the west or the passenger pigeon of the east. And as we could mimic the birds, we could also mimic the function of the large herds that once roamed in great numbers across the grasslands. It was a vision of reinvigorating the forestlands by mimicking the diversity of the layers from the ground all the way to the canopy.

This form of agriculture, I would later learn, was expressed in the term *permaculture*, an approach based on natural ecosystems observed when founder Bill Mollison was working in forests of Tasmania as a naturalist. I would also find there was a similar system specific to grasslands based on the interplay of predator, prey, and plants such as those I had observed in the meadows of Idaho watching the wolves hunting elk. This system was coined *Holistic Management* and was founded in Africa's savannah by Allan Savory after years of working with native trackers and as a wildlife ecologist. Holistic Management created a blueprint for reversing desertification of grasslands.

Even though I didn't know the terms *permaculture* and *Holistic Management* yet, I'd come to my own understanding that we needed systems of agriculture and of living that mimicked and took wisdom from the wild. It was in nature where I found solace, a balm for my despair, and where I found hope for the rejuvenation of life on earth. I realized that this was what Gilbert was talking about when he spoke about nature healing people mentally. If I could be part of bringing back nature as the pillar to education and to the built environment, then simply by design, education and our built environment would have the power to heal. There was not any mystic outside force that would reverse the actions of human-caused climate disasters. The answers to the world's crisis lay within the design of nature herself.

Part Two

Food

M y great-grandparents homesteaded near Flathead Lake, Montana. They farmed their food according to the bountiful resources nature provided. The topsoil was deep and rich like chocolate mousse, ready to accept any seed that landed upon its freshly tilled surface. The homesteads in the area were diverse, providing for a full diet. Bees, vegetables, milk and beef cows, pigs, and chickens all coexisted on the homestead, to be consumed by the family or sold at the farm store. The need for survival and a comfortable, independent life drove the decisions. America held promise of limitless bounty for immigrants of the early twentieth century, like my great-grandparents, who came from County Cork, Ireland. America was a place where virgin forests still stretched out beyond the horizon, and game was so plentiful that what was not raised on the homestead could be easily hunted on the surrounding prairie.

The homesteaders, such as my great-grandparents, who

were seeking a better life and the Indigenous people who were faced with racism posed a juxtaposition which marked the era. I loved the simple way of life my grandmother would speak of, yet I knew the dark history the Homestead Act was founded upon. Prior to homesteading, smallpox outbreaks ravaged Indigenous populations; the Salish and Pend d'Oreille bands of Montana, where my family homesteaded, were reduced by one-half to three-quarters. Other Indigenous people in the Northwest who were infected with the smallpox disease were even forced by police to return to their villages, carrying the disease to the rest of their tribe in an act of genocide by the settlers (Lange 2003).

The racism continued, and prior to the land on the Flathead Reservation being offered to white homesteaders, treaties were written and broken, bison were massacred, and Indigenous lands continued to shrink. The Flathead Reservation allotments went to the tribes first, with each family getting a set amount of land. That allowed the supposed surplus lands to be opened up to white homesteaders, which resulted in a loss of 60 percent of the reservation land (Juneau 2010).

My grandmother's parents had been some of those waiting in line for the reservation land to open up for settlement. I listened to my grandmother as she would proudly tell me all about her life growing up on the Montana homestead. Her stories about the plot of land at the base of the Mission Mountains were vivid, and when she told them to me, as we sat drinking lemonade, I felt I was there with her. Her parents had moved from Ireland during the potato famine to Butte, Montana, to work in the copper mines for $3.50 a day. She would speak of the mining work that eventually led to her father's sickness and death.

"He worked all day in those hot mines, sweating in his clothes. When he would surface at the end of the day into the below-freezing temperatures of Montana to make the long walk home, his clothes would freeze to his body," she told me. "When your great-grandfather saw an announcement in the paper that land in the Flathead Indian Reservation was going to be offered to homesteaders, he jumped at the opportunity to own his own piece of land in America. Your great-grandparents filed for 120 acres and started homesteading in 1912. They gathered up a horse, a spring wagon, two milk cows, household goods, and everything they thought they would need to get a start on a piece of land."

Grammy looked lost in thought, as she was reliving another time. I listened intently, wanting to hear every detail, and also wondering if her parents knew of the broken treaties they were benefiting from. "They took a train nearly two hundred miles from Butte to a little town called Dixon. From there they loaded everything they could in the spring wagon and drove the cattle eight miles from Dixon to the homestead."

It was hard to imagine. "What did they do once they got to the homestead?" I asked Grammy.

"Well," she said slowly, "they had five years to prove up on the land. That meant they had to put a fence around it, build a shelter, and make improvements. Your great-grandfather would leave in the winters to go to British Columbia to work in the mines to make extra money, while my mother, your great-grandmother, would stay home to take care of the children and the homestead. We would sell the raw milk from our Holstein cows to the nearby towns to help pay the bills.

"Nine children." Grammy paused and put a hand on my knee. "My mother gave birth to four boys and five girls. When my father was hospitalized, she held the family and homestead together. I was the youngest and it was my job to do the milking in the early morning before school and in the evening when I returned home. I could never miss a day. We also had a vegetable garden, honeybees, some beef cattle, and horses. I walked out our front door and we had a store to the left of the steps where we sold what we did not eat from the homestead."

When she spoke of the homestead life she had a look of pride on her face—a look that I realized much later in my life, when I became an adult, comes when hard work and perseverance result in great accomplishment. I was in awe of the subsistence-based way of life my grandmother lived.

"When the Great Depression came in 1929 and the stock market crashed, it did not bother my family much because we didn't own stocks," she told me. "We were able to make do with what we grew on the farm and made money selling the surplus. Your great-grandfather was always coming up with new ideas. He started a cream delivery route, picking up the cream from the nearby farmers and delivering it to the creamery. He got paid one cent for each pound of butterfat from the farmer and the creamery." The far-off look I saw in my grandmother's eyes when she spoke about the homestead made me wish I was born in a different era, so I too, could experience what she had. "Every day we would walk two miles to school. In the winter there would sometimes be three feet of snow on the ground."

Even though my grandmother had traded all the harsh winters and hardships of the homestead for a comfortable life as a nurse married to an air force pilot, the values and work ethic of being raised so close to the land, with the constant reminder of where her food and shelter came from, were instilled deep inside her being. As I sat there listening to my grandmother, the idea of life on the homestead, having milk cows, horses, and the great expanse of Montana foothills, conjured up a desire inside me to live close to the land and grow my own food where rivers and mountains were met with endless sky.

This abundance of food was not a result of the lack of humans. It was the opposite. The tribes that occupied all the land across the west prior to settlement did not just passively reap the benefits of plants and animals. They intentionally pruned, weeded, seeded, selectively harvested, and tilled. They learned from the grizzly bear who, when digging for and eating mature bulbs, scattered the bulbets that were propagated from the larger bulb, thereby aiding multiple new plants in the process of harvesting others for food. They learned from the scrub jay, who helped oaks reproduce by losing track of some of the acorns they buried. The ingenuity of the Indigenous people of the region stewarding the land directly benefited the homestead families.

For settlers like my great-grandparents, living rurally and knowing how to grow food to feed a family was freedom, a way to escape the bondage of the coal mines or manufacturing plants. No longer working for the benefit of another man's wealth, the homesteaders gained their own salvation by staking their claim. But that claim ended up becoming an escape from one source of greed and extraction toward another. Early twentieth-century farmers and ranchers were driven by an agriculture ethos of expansion and accumulation of land and wealth. The original sense of autonomy and freedom from having to earn money eventually led to the tilling of expansive prairies for wheat, with the dollar as the main motivator every time.

As agribusiness grew profitable, the well-intentioned family homesteaders like my relatives got pushed out. Farms shifted from families growing enough for their own needs and sharing the surplus with neighbors, to much larger and, ironically, less productive farms. Export was on the rise. Wealth from the farm income was becoming centralized to fewer farm owners, which sent the next generation fleeing off the farm and into the cities. In the mid-eighteen hundreds, the majority of Americans were farmers. In the early nineteen hundreds, 40 percent were farmers. By the end of the twentieth century, 2.5 percent were farmers ("Historical Timeline" 2017). As the percentage of Americans who farmed dwindled, so did the soils—removed from the prairie as fast as a jackrabbit racing a grassfire. The world's greatest grasslands were raped and pillaged of their protective coat of soil by the plow, killing the ecology of the microbes. These microbes, such as bacteria, fungi, and nematodes, form the relationships with the plants that allow them to absorb nutrients and resist drought, disease, and pests. Farming those bountiful lands first brought immense wealth, but those extractive techniques created the terrorizing dust storms leading into the Great Depression.

The homesteading life I pictured when my grandmother told me her stories was a far cry from the farm exploitation that eventually led to the environmental crisis of present and future generations. I yearned to produce, hunt, and gather the food I consumed, but I was separated by two generations from my homesteading family. Things had gone really wrong with agriculture during the age of industrialization, after the home-steading era. The native soil and the Indigenous people were removed, and I would come to find out that the two were in-terlinked. Indigenous peoples had been tending to the wild in a very intentional way. The plant life on the prairie depended on the intentional disturbance and tending from the large herds of bison and other hooved animals as well as the early humans who played a part in the predator-prey-plant relationship. Once the land tenders and herds were removed, the prairie lan-guished. Over-hunting of bison and plowing the prairie by the settlers was in stark contrast to the natural cycles of life.

I posed a question to myself. How was I to play the role of steward to the land and people while maintaining respect for all life and treating all living things as my relatives? The idea of viewing all life around as kin, that nature includes humans, describes *kincentric ecology*. The term, developed by Enrique Salmón, describes the Indigenous view that humans are an integral part of the complexity of life (Salmón 2000). Salmón is from the culture of the Rarámuri, commonly known as the Tarahumara people. They live in northern Mexico's Sierra Madre Occidental mountain range. This region remains one of the most biologically diverse regions in the world. The people have continued to flourish with their traditional lifestyle by following land ethics that restore abundance to their food source: they gather only a bushel of a plant and leave the rest, or avoid collecting plants if their numbers are sparse in one location, instead finding the right location for gathering. There is an understanding within the people that all life has breath and that breath is shared with all relatives—both human and non-human. Within this shared breath comes the caretaking spirit and the knowledge that health of one's own mind, body, and spirit is directly linked to the health of the natural world. As Oren Lyons, the faith keeper of the Onondaga, so eloquently put it, "What you people call your natural resources, our people call our relatives."

There are different ways to gain sustenance from the land. One way is regenerative and comes with an understanding that every time we eat, a life is taken, whether plant or animal, and *we can give more life than we take*. Soil and biodiversity thrive as a result. This life is treated with reverence, and the fertility is returned after the take. The nutrients not absorbed by a person are returned to the land. A bison eats this way, whether it knows it or not. The act of its biting the grass sword adds vigor to the perennial plant by keeping it free from rot and ruin. Enough of the plant is left to absorb the rays of sunlight for regrowth, like a coppiced willow that continues to shoot up new growth, absorbing water from the depths of the soil. As long as the plant is disturbed with a cut or a bite, it will continue to flourish. Once that disturbance is gone, that plant will languish.

The bison were perfectly adapted for life on the enormous prairie, having prehistoric relatives enduring for hundreds of thousands of years (Callenbach 1996). The bison in return became food for many predators, including humans. The hunted bison, which at one time roamed in such great numbers they could be compared to the herds on the Serengeti, returned minerals back into the soil in the form of blood, bones, feces, and urine. The humans and other predators gained healthy bodies from this nutrient-dense meat and also returned the minerals from their own excrement back into the soils.

Predators were necessary for the survival of the bison herds, weeding out the weak and sick in order to make the whole herd stronger. Predators were also necessary for the health of the grass. They kept the herds moving and bunched up for survival. The bison then arranged themselves in high density, yet only stayed in one area for a short duration, which excited all the life beneath their hooves. When they moved on for fear of being hunted, what they left was food for the life above and below the ground in the form of manure. The bison then did not return to that patch of prairie until that land and those plants had a chance to recover, before the dance happened again. It was as if a divine force were orchestrating the relationships between bison and grass, hunter and hunted, death and birth. I longed to bring back this sacred full-circle food system.

Unfortunately, most of us procure food in an extractive way. When I traveled the country as a teen I saw vast prairies plowed under to grow soybeans reliant on chemical inputs, making the farms toxic to anyone nearby. The chemicals transfer into the body through drift and dust, and children who live in proximity to crops sprayed with pesticides and herbicides show traces of the chemicals in their urine (Ward et al. 2006). I witnessed the torture of confinement livestock yards that stretched along the highways in Central California with excrement instead of feeding soil, creating limitless waste and pollution. This form of farming, driven by greed and heavily dependent on fossil fuels, government subsidies, and external inputs, led to a deep grief inside me. My own diet growing up had been supplemented with what our family grew in our garden or what I foraged from the wild plants, but it largely consisted of the foods purchased from a grocery. With the simple act of eating foods from a grocery store, I had been treating the earth as if it were a trash can that I could discard garbage into whenever I wanted. The consequence of this ignorance was out of sight, like when the garbage truck comes to take the trash to *away*. With this realization of my own tainted food source, tribulation beyond measure was brewing inside me. I longed to shift the destructive past into an optimistic future, where humans could once again give more than we received.

In this search I found myself drawn to Indigenous cultures, whose transition to eating foods cultivated in rows was not a welcomed change. Reservation lands in the United States did not provide abundant wild food so the food culture shifted for survival, not out of choice. In these tribes the shift was within the last two hundred years instead of my own ancestry, in which the change from hunter-gather peoples happened thousands of years prior. The history was similar across the world, whether Ireland or North America. People from another land came with the tools of extraction and conquered the Indigenous peoples. A dramatic shift in land use resulted.

I needed to go to a place where ancestral pride ran deep, where people did not hold themselves separate from the earth, but where their relationship with the earth determined the meaning of their existence, the peace inside their heart, and well-being of all their kin. I knew that those who settled this continent, my ancestors, killed or sickened the Indigenous peoples, leading to their massive decline. The Indigenous families who still remained were forced to conform to the settlers' way of life. I felt a drive to recompense the victims of that destruction by learning from them and offering my help, in the form of hands ready to work.

My biggest transition with food came when I was sixteen and I was invited by a Lakota family to the Pine Ridge Indian Reservation. I drove into the reservation and saw poverty similar to what I had seen in Mexico and other poor countries. The streets were lined with piles of trash and junk cars. Broken plastic toys sprawled on the lawns, and many of the windows in the houses were broken and boarded up. At the entrance lay a casino, a large new building with bright lights and all the modern architecture of a wealthy California city. Yet within the reservation the infrastructure looked as if the people were on the brink of survival.

The land around was desolate. Grey, cracked dirt lay fallow with occasional bunches of sage and sparse grass. In the 1870s the Lakota had been forced away from their land in the Black Hills onto the Pine Ridge Indian Reservation. The land that was designated as the reservation was not the hunting ground that once sustained the people. It was not the fertile places where the Lakota once lived and harvested roots and plants. With the bison hunted to near extinction by the settlers, the Lakota could not feed their family in the traditional way. They were not farmers; nor were they looking to set a plow to the soil to plant crops. They were hunter-gatherers.

I was invited to stay with the Peters family in their house

on a neighborhood street about five blocks from the small town of Pine Ridge.

The Peters family's dwelling was a typical single-story house, with a small yard out front, a carport, and small windows. The design seemed less functional as I opened the door and the large family, including extended relatives, sat in every corner of every room. A young woman sat on the couch, only to jump up when she heard the cry of her baby down the hall. In the kitchen, separated by a wall from the living room, I heard the bustling of women and an earthy smell like garden soil wafting from the stove.

I rounded the corner to see a group of women chopping up potatoes. Lena Peters greeted me with a warm smile and a big hug. Setting down my pack, I got right to work. Knife in hand, I watched the women work rapidly as they chatted and I tried to follow suit, cutting the smooth brown potatoes just as they did. The chatter was lively and I had a difficult time keeping up with the conversation. A brown liquid simmered in a large pot on the stove, where I put the chopped potatoes once they were done. Large chunks of meat and bone emerged from the bubbling liquid as I scraped the potatoes from the cutting board. The smell permeated the air, drawing people in the kitchen to peer in to see what was cooking.

My cultural differences became overwhelmingly clear, especially over food. On my first evening in the house, the family was in the kitchen laughing and sharing a meal together. I was alone in my room eating my peanut butter and toast, separated from the stories I wanted to hear, from the family I wanted to be welcomed into. Why? I had never eaten beef. My mother had ingrained into my very being the images of cattle standing in a cramped feedlot filled with their own feces and urine, with no defense from their incarceration. I could not bring myself to stab my fork into the flesh of an animal who was subject to mistreatment due to the greed of humans.

Will Peters, the father of the family, asked why I was not eating with the family. It was their tradition that everyone who came was fed and welcomed to the table. I explained that I had never eaten beef because of the way the animals were treated. He looked at me crossly.

Will explained to me, "We are honoring the lives of the animals by eating them. When you eat the meat, that animal becomes part of you and gives you strength." Though he was usually a very gentle and caring man, he spoke in a harsh tone. He went on to say, "These animals were put on this earth by the Great Spirit to nourish our people."

Not eating the food that was offered was foreign and offensive to him and caused disconnect in our understanding of one another. I had become a separated idealist by letting my own past experiences become prejudices toward other people and their experiences.

As the evening progressed, the activities were jovial and I joined the family. The next day was the annual pow-wow on the reservation. The children in the house were preparing for dancing, drumming, and singing as they glided around practicing their acts. There was a lot of activity as the girls opened the closets to pull out their dresses and moccasins in preparation. The girls, even the smallest of toddlers just learning to walk, adorned themselves with the most beautiful dresses that hung long, decorated with beads and colorful fabric. Shawls hung over their shoulders with long fringe dangling down over their dresses resembling upside-down grass waving in the wind as they glided across the linoleum floor. From the closet came feathered fans and moccasins that were set out to adorn the house like handmade displays of art. Intricate patterns of turtles with decorative shells, diamond shapes, and patterns of blues, reds, white, greens, and black were beaded into the buckskin. It was a preparation for a big day of the gathering of nations.

The next day, people gathered from across the reservation and beyond for dancing and singing. On the pow-wow grounds, a large circle was set up in an open field. Surrounding the circle was a shade arbor made of pine poles with cedar boughs laid on top in a lattice for shade. Off to one side, a group of men and boys sat around a large drum, singing and beating the stretched rawhide in unison, each with their own long, padded drumstick. The people in the round arena surrounded by the shade arbor danced and never missed a beat. I watched the elders engrossed in the dance. It looked as if there was nothing surrounding them, no spectators or judges, just the next step in front of them and the rhythm of the dance. The dancers looked and moved like the animal they were dancing. They danced the deer, with legs rising up high in a celebratory bound. The costumes were full of eagle feathers, buckskin filled with beadwork of all things natural: bears, horses, turtles, and butterflies. Watching the dancing and listening to the traditional songs inspired genuine gratitude in me for the earth. It was as if everyone were celebrating something big, like surviving a harsh winter.

Off to the side of the arbor, a young girl taught me the grass dance. We swayed our bodies like the tall grass on the prairie while she sang. I pictured the grass bending in the wind and bouncing back up again, never breaking at the force but rather being flexible and resilient. It seemed clear to me the way the little girl was dancing that she had seen the way the grass dances on the vast prairie with the wind as the choreographer and the grass as a million dancers all taking their place on stage. The pow-wow eventually came to a close, but that was not the last time on that trip I would visit an arbor where ceremony was held.

The following weekend, I was invited to attend a thank-you ceremony conducted by a family who had their prayers for their sick child to be well again answered. I sat in a circle with the Peters family as their cousins from a nearby town offered their thank-you or giveaway ceremony, called a *Wopila*. As we stood in the arbor of the ceremony grounds, the family hosting the Wopila brought out large crates of beautiful star quilts, useful kitchen tools, books, and toys. The gifts were abundant, both lovely and useful. The family putting on the ceremony had had their prayers answered, so this was a way to give back and say Wopila—thank you.

The family passed out food that was sacred to their people. It was food that was not just nourishing but healing medicine. Feeling the soft, greasy mash, brown with flecks of red and white, in a bowl that was passed to me, I grasped a pinch between my fingers and lifted it to my lips. The sweet smell of chokecherries combined with a rich, earthy smell wafted toward me. As the food entered my mouth, a shot ran through my body like lightning, striking through me to the earth to recharge and restore the earth-atmosphere electrical balance. This was *Wasna* (pemmican), made of ground-up bison, bone marrow, and chokecherries. It was the sacred traditional food for healing during ceremonies. As I ate the Wasna I felt what Will had taught me about the animals becoming part of me. I ate the sacred food and pictured the land where the chokecherries were gathered. I pictured the grasses that according to Lakota belief were put on this earth to feed the bison.

The Peterses believed so strongly that the ceremonies needed to come back, and they live their ways despite the tragedy of their people being displaced and imprisoned. I spent time with that family, got to know where their hearts were and how important it was for them to continue to pass on their heritage in a meaningful way to the next generation. I sat and I ate bison with their family. My peanut butter and bread languished in my backpack.

I knew now why the Peters family reached for the packages of meat at the supermarket, holding on to any thread of the past they could. Their ancestors were taken from their hunting ground and put on that reservation, far from the fertile valleys where their people had flourished. With the large herds of mega fauna gone, the desert had engulfed them. The prairie suffered when the keystone species such as the bison and wolves were removed. It became a desert of the kind where the cracked, parched earth is sparsely covered in sagebrush and a kangaroo rat scurries from one bush to the next in a mad dash to make it to cover. There is so much bare ground that even North America's smallest falcon, the American kestrel, needs to watch his food source or that too will be depleted like the rest of the species on the barren ground.

In the desolate, remote landscape of the reservation, the only option for food was that of the convenient, cheap, and easy-to-ship variety. What, then, was the next step in unraveling this situation? It was like the Peters family had been given an ugly sweater that did not fit and they were forced to wear it. Their original ways and their bison kin were no longer part of an intact ecological web, yet any thread to the past, like traditional recipes prepared with supermarket ingredients, was a spark of hope for the future.

I sat looking out the window into the darkness one morning after returning from the reservation. The looming memories of the dreams I'd been having since the age of fourteen came to mind. In those dreams I walked amongst dead bodies after a war. Each watering hole I came across had dried up. In the distance, cities were up in flames.

Those dreams were coming true. Rain no longer falls in vast desert landscapes. There is no water for the crops, as the water table has dropped nearly out of reach of a drill. Desertification has stricken many parts of the world, leading to war-torn communities whose only choice is flee to unwelcoming lands. Gilbert Walking Bull told me of a vision he had that a yellow gas would come, killing many people. He said it was only the ones who know how to live like the wild animals who will survive.

This Lakota community I was invited into looked from the outside as though they did not have much—yet they gave me plenty. They welcomed and fed me, taught me their traditions and ceremonies, and never asked for anything in return. Throughout my life, I have visited other Indigenous tribes who shared those same values. Even if they have just a little, they always share it.

After spending time on the reservation, and being at the pow-wow and Wopila, I took inside a way of being that the dancers embodied with the dance. It was not what they said or how they looked, but how they interacted with one another that shifted something inside of me. It was the act of living in prayer. They believed that sending one's mind to the spirit world to ask for help in living a good life with meaning was a necessity for survival. Consistently, the sacred was acknowledged and held as a pillar that supported the entire community. For me, this acknowledgment that all life is sacred brought me a deeper sense of belonging and connection to the life around me.

I was still tracking animals voraciously at the time, and I brought this way of being with the sacred into the trail. Tracking became my dance. At times when I tracked I would go to a place and picture in my mind the animal I wanted to track, say a thanksgiving and a prayer, the way I had learned from the Lakota, and do a dance for that animal. I used my feet as drumsticks and the earth as a large drum, matching my rhythm with the rhythm of the earth like an elder I had seen in the pow-wow ring. However hunched and frail, he still embodied the energy of the deer he was dancing. I let go of the clock that kept so many stuck to a schedule based on a false reality and opened up my body as a radar, surrendering to the subtlest of sensations from the land.

The grass dance the little girl taught me, as well as those I witnessed at the pow-wow, were part of the culture of hunting and gathering. Relating to life through the dance created empathy toward the animals hunted and the plants gathered. I understood then why it was so important to keep those dances alive. By dancing, the Peters family and their community could still tap into their ancestral way of life.

Growing up we ate shellfish gathered in the ocean and inlets. We ate fish when we knew where it was from. We did not eat anything with four legs. I remember as a little girl going through the grocery store holding onto my mother's pant leg, peering out to see those packages of meat in the display case, all red and bloody with plastic covering them on a little Styrofoam tray bearing no resemblance to their original form. We never reached down for those packages. We did not eat animals that were not able to be free like the fish in the ocean. This shaped my view of food. I proudly stated my food status during school lunches or at sleepovers. I enjoyed being different. Having knowledge of food gave me power.

Before my wilderness training, when I was traveling as a teenage vagabond, I became vegan to protest the cruelty of animals in confinement and the chemicals that were used in the leather industry. I did not want any part of the chromium leather tanning which replaced plant or animal tanning and was more often than not done in poor countries where the carcinogenic chemical ended up contaminating nearby bodies of water, not to mention the bodies of the workers. I also did not want to be part of the industrialized agriculture system, where nutrients were being eroded at an unprecedented rate. Soils once rich with organic matter, minerals, and nutrients were replaced with synthetic fertilizers applied at such a large scale that it leached into the groundwater, contaminated the water, and suffocated aquatic life. As long as I did not have to actually work or do anything physical, I could deplete my body of those foods that were derived directly from animals. But the vegan diet took its toll on my body in a short time. My energy was depleted and my eyes sunken from the nutrients I was missing out on by avoiding animal fats and protein. I slept a lot. When I returned from a trip, my mother saw that my eyes had dark circles under them. I was malnourished. She quickly cooked me a meal of fish and eggs that boosted me back to health and marked the end of my vegan lifestyle.

I felt that the monocultures of our modern Western human lives were echoed in our food. The row crops grown and shipped were like the lines of young adults waiting for a degree just to be trucked to some unknown destination beyond their will. I had seen the agricultural fields of the open plains as I traveled the country. The fertile valleys where bison once roamed were now engulfed in crops of corn and soy laid out in lines as straight as jet streams as far as the eye could see. What made people stop caring about producing food for their own basic needs? It felt as if no one even cared about the food they put in their mouths, where it came from, how many lives were destroyed in the process, or what it did to their very own bodies. Food for people was the latest addiction; we were living for the next quick fix, not fully understanding the consequences.

Finding the foods aligned with my values and my body's energy requirements became my primary motive throughout my teenage years. After trying out every diet from vegan to paleo, after wasting away without animal protein and then tasting the electric nutrition of pemmican, I held a vision of my own perfect diet. This was one where I grew my own food like my homesteading great-grandparents had, one where what I did not grow I would supplement from the wild plants and animals that surrounded me. Each one of these foods I consumed would come from a source that regenerated the earth's soils instead of depleting them. I wanted my food choices to be good for the earth I loved: I wanted to be a regenetarian.

When I had stepped out of the wilderness after my clothes caught on fire, I felt a calling to find a regenerative solution to humans living on this earth. Any other path felt like suicide for the entire human species. When Gilbert Walking Bull spoke of the time that would come when the humans who knew how to live like the wild animals would survive, he always had one caveat: The visions he received from the spirits were in spirit time. He could not translate the spirit time to calendar years. Running into the wilderness and waiting for the earth to come to an end from the destruction caused by my own species would be selfish and unproductive. A fire was ignited in me that night at Cedar Falls when I surrendered myself to the elements. I became aware that my vision was part of a solution, one where people learned to adapt to the ever-changing ecosystem and find ways to live abundant lives while at the same time restoring abundance in earth's life forms. And now food and agriculture became paramount in that vision.

Becoming a regenetarian meant treating food as sacred medicine like the pemmican and creating more life whenever a life was taken, whether plant or animal. I needed to start to think like a tender of the prairie.

Permaculture

John Muir wrote in his diary, "Like the Indians, we ought to know how to get the starch out of fern and saxifrage stalks, lily bulbs, pine bark, etc. Our education has been sadly neglected for many generations" (Muir 1911).

Like Muir, I felt as though I was catching up to an in-depth knowledge of nature and how to apply my hands to stewardship. Once I finished with my high school wilderness immersion, I continued to track, and I traveled to teach groups of people who were starting their own nature schools to mimic Wilderness Awareness School. Our little group of teenagers became a global movement. We were like grass seeds in the wind, carrying a message around the globe of something that was possible when humans were allowed to follow their full potential.

At nineteen years old, working as an instructor for Wilderness Awareness School, I traveled to Northern California to teach a class on the language of birds organized by a non-profit land trust in the Santa Cruz Mountains. I found myself in a melting pot of people from very different backgrounds and cultures, all in one room, aligned with similar visions to my own. Amongst the students and helpers were a modern witch by the name of Starhawk, a naturalist by the name of Scott Brinton, several biologists, and people from various grassroots non-profits doing good work for the planet and humanity. Many of these people were up on the latest innovations of organic farming, community living, and modern-day homesteading.

It was here where I first heard the term *permaculture*, when people were introducing themselves around the circle. Starhawk called herself a permaculture designer and witch. The naturalist, Scott, said he also built permaculture gardens for kids at an outdoor school. I found out that permaculture is based on the patterns and mutually beneficial relationships observed in nature. Permaculture applies these observations in nature to human-designed farms and dwellings. This was so intriguing to me—I felt a surge of energy pulse through my body and chills down my spine when I heard the people in the class speak of their work in permaculture. This was what I had been seeking: a design system where I could have a hand in growing abundant, nutritious food while at the same time treating all life as my relatives. And it already existed! There were people I could learn these systems from!

One evening at the bird language course, over dinner, I met Gary Riekes, founder of the Riekes Center for Human

Enhancement. With bushy eyebrows and a big smile, he wore a hooded sweatshirt and cap with Stanford Football across the front. Along with naturalist Scott Brinton, Gary had recently added a nature awareness department to his athletic fitness and creative arts center as a way for students to connect with themselves in the healing environment of nature. Gary offered me a place to live on his nearby property in the Santa Cruz Mountains in exchange for helping to start a field research center for the Riekes Center Nature Awareness program. Each student that entered the Riekes Center went through a transformational program focusing on their individual goals and aspirations. The center provided opportunities for diverse participants in the program to foster their passions. In order to bring inspiration back to their respective sport or art, he wanted them to also have an outlet to express passions for the natural world and gain insight by being in nature. Of course I took him up on his offer. I had fallen in love with the water-shed where his land was nestled when I'd visited in previous years with the Wilderness Awareness School. The Bay Area was a hotbed for permaculture, so I packed my bags and moved to the small rural coastal town of San Gregorio.

While living in California, I continued to track wolves in Idaho in the summers and take trips around the world to teach tracking and nature awareness with the Wilderness Awareness School staff. I also worked tracking mountain lions for a local non-profit land trust, Peninsula Open Space Trust, in the Santa Cruz Mountains. As a tracker for hire, I had entered into the realm of influencing decisions made by the people who stewarded lands with the goal of enhancing habitat for the creatures I loved—the creatures that had shaped who I was and taught me some of my biggest lessons in life. I located fresh tracks and signs of a mountain lion on the land trust preserve south of San Francisco and set up cameras to capture the images of these wild creatures that moved in and out of the suburban neighborhood undetected. I was to map out their travel routes in order to influence where trails and roads would be built with minimal impact on the animals.

I studied permaculture in every minute of my spare time. Permaculture blended what I had learned on the organic farm, what I learned at WAS, and the lessons I'd learned from Indigenous people. Permaculture provided solutions to the problems I had seen in my travels. In *Permaculture: A Designers' Manual* by Bill Mollison, I found a page that read: "The Prime Directive of Permaculture: The only ethical decision is to take responsibility for our own existence and that of our children's....It is a philosophy of working with rather than against nature; of protracted and thoughtful observation rather than protracted and thoughtless action; of looking at systems and people in all their functions, rather than asking only one yield of them; and of allowing systems to demonstrate their own evolution." (Mollison 1998) In its very definition, permaculture is a way to build agriculturally productive ecosystems that have the resiliency of natural ecosystems. The root words of *permaculture*, a term developed in the 1970s by

David Holmgren and Bill Mollison, are *permanent agriculture* or *permanent culture*. In permaculture practice, by integrating land and people providing people with food, water, shelter, and other needs, abundance is created and the surplus is shared with all living species. I was hooked. Someone had, through direct observation of nature, actually created a road map for living harmoniously with all life and laid out a way of being part of the solution to the devastation of the centuries since colonization.

A few months after I settled into living in California, I took a few days off of tracking mountain lions and working at the Riekes field station and drove up to meet a couple renowned for their permaculture gardens. I had been waiting to experience with all my senses a permaculture landscape like those I had been reading about. Driving the long road out to the little agriculture town of Point Reyes Station, I was greeted by a woman called Penny Livingston. With long silvery hair, Penny had a face that showed her experience. When she smiled her full-toothed smile, crow's feet deepened beside her eyes, showing that she'd spent a lot of time with that expression. We had the smiling in common at the least. Penny and I had corresponded prior to meeting and she knew I had a love of tracking and nature, so she took me out for a drive to the nearby Point Reyes National Seashore. The landmass demarking the sanctuary jutted out from the coast between Tomales Bay, Drakes Bay, and the Pacific Ocean, marked by the tectonic plate of the San Andreas Fault.

As we drove, Penny told me of a program she was developing. It was a training that blended the skills of permaculture with nature observation. The Regenerative Design Institute, as she called this new project, would rewire the brains of people who sought these types of trainings by immersing them in nature and permaculture to develop healthy and abundant livelihoods that would enhance fertility and biodiversity on the planet. She would take a select group of students and train them for a year. During that time they would design and develop a living system based on permaculture ethics and principles. This training was very intriguing to me.

Riding along in her station wagon, I scanned the landscape. We passed through large stands of Douglas fir trees mixed with California bay laurel and coast live oak. As we drove, she told me of the Coast Miwok peoples who once tended these wildlands. They kept the grasslands open for hunting by using fire, resulting in a better food source for the herds of elk and pronghorn and open visible hunting grounds for the tribes. She went on to explain that the herds of tule elk once reached one thousand strong in one herd alone. The elk and the Coast Miwok were in a dance with one another. The people kept the food source abundant for the elk and in return the elk were hunted. She explained to me that there was a park reintroduction effort of the elk, but that the dance between the predators, the elk, and the humans no longer existed. Not only were the people not consciously tending their food source, but also the predators, such as the California grizzly bear, who once frequented the California coast were extinct.

The consequence of this is that the elk become entangled in a political battle and the land does not see the historic benefits from the presence of the elk because their traditional migratory patterns are interrupted with fences and lack of land. Their behavior changes without predators keeping pressure on the herd to continue moving to fresh grasslands. This results in overgrazing of plants, and left unchecked will populate until there is no food source left, resulting in a larger die-off of the herds. The reintroduction of the elk, along with other forms of management of the parkland, was a political mess, creating fragmentation amongst the different groups of people. The ranchers and farmers who grazed cattle on the grasslands and raised oysters in the bay, the politicians who made decisions at the capital but who lacked any connection to the place, and the two million people who visited the park every year were all at odds with each other and the future of the parkland. Penny explained that the grasslands do much better with grazing animals, whether cattle or elk, but that observant humans need to play a vital role in the design and interaction of these systems if they are to be ecologically functional. This concept was just starting to sink in for me—that cattle could play the role that elk once played as long as there was intentional management and a way to mimic the actions of the predators that were now extinct.

As we entered the grassland, we started sharing our observations with each other. She pointed out the trail of water gaining velocity as it traveled across the land. The trail was worn smooth from the water picking up any small pebble that may have lain there. Penny said the traveling water could be captured or routed in a way that would allow it to penetrate the soil or be stored for later use. She pointed out that once the water hit the road, it picked up even more speed until it gushed out along the downward-sloping edge, causing the erosion she showed me. She was tracking water!

I stopped to part the grass and noticed a bobcat trail that led along the edge of the water trail. I pointed it out to Penny. The bobcat had been using the edge of the water trail but was hidden by the tall grass.

As we traveled along, Penny was looking at the soil types. She would point out the clay soils. "Those would be perfect for natural building materials!" she exclaimed.

We continued to drive down the road on the edge of the grassland. The ocean appeared in the distance. Penny pointed out the trees flagged by the winds, indicating the prevailing wind direction. I spotted a well-used game trail and asked her to pull over. There before us were tule elk tracks crossing the road, filing in one behind the next to travel through the grasslands. They looked fresh, lacking moisture on the disturbed surface, indicating they were not weathered from the morning's fog. I asked if she wanted to follow the tracks and she eagerly agreed.

The tracks led us over a rise in the grasslands. Quietly we walked until we got up to a ridge. There before us stood a massive bull elk surrounded by five cow elk. With his neck outstretched and muzzle turned up, he sounded an eerie whistle out of his slightly open mouth. His dark brown neck, with long hairs reaching from chin to chest, flared as he bugled to communicate with the cow elk as well as any bulls that may have been lurking nearby. The dark neck transmuted into a light brown body with a whitish rump. The small group did not compare to the one-thousand-head-strong herds of the past, but still held the magnificence of a species communicating with each other in a way that each individual understood and vocalized in response. The small group sounded high-pitched calls in response to one another, keeping their group together and communicating any alarm. It was an orchestra that needed no rehearsals.

As we stood in amazement in the presence of these magnificent creatures, I could see Penny's eyes scanning the grasslands. I asked her what she was seeing and she pointed out the types of grasses the elk were feasting upon. The native perennial bunch-grasses dotting the trail looked delicate and wispy amongst the non-native annual grasses. The grasses had already dispersed their seeds, leaving a protective shell opened and exposed, like a mother without a child. She said next year she would come back to that patch once the grass was ready to harvest and collect the seed for her land. I would never have registered that patch of productive purple needle grass or noticed that it would be a site to collect the seeds to propagate elsewhere. Aside from working on the organic farm, I had never focused on propagation of anything in the wild. That day I was walking with Penny, I was focused on propagation of observations and collection of data. Collecting wild seeds was a new concept.

The things Penny focused on showed me how she perceived the world. I had seen the trail of the bobcat in the grass and parted the grasses because I knew there was a good chance I would find the tracks of a bobcat traveling along the edge of the trail, seeking cover in the tall grass. The bobcat could stalk up on the small mammals living in the cover of the plants while at the same time remaining hidden from larger predators or people. I knew what to look for, after having followed the tracks of that species for countless hours. Penny had focused on the movement of water and the types of soil with similar intensity. She had spent her own countless hours observing the way water traveled, was directed or dissipated, absorbed or shed. She applied all of that information to her landscape.

As we drove along, we buzzed like honeybees after being so close to those majestic elk. Our observations were flowing as if our brains had opened up to each other. I realized I had been viewing the earth through the eyes of a non-human animal—I'd worked immensely hard to understand how to get in the mindset of a bobcat, a beaver, a deer, a wolf. And now it was time for me to view the land through the eyes of a human animal—a responsible one, holding all living beings as my kin and relatives. I had learned, as Gilbert Walking Bull prophesized, how to live like the wild animals. I felt I needed to re-learn, or perhaps even reimagine, what it meant to be human.

As we approached the neighborhood streets of Point Reyes Station after spending the day out reading the landscape, we pulled into Penny's driveway. Opening the large wooden gate that separated her house and yard from the street, I stepped into a utopia full of life suited for both human and nature. It was nearing dinnertime and I was very hungry from both the physical and mental strain of the day's activities. But that seemed less important as I feasted my senses on her garden. I walked slowly, looking, while Penny unloaded a few items from her car. I had never seen anything like this before. Every plant I walked past was cultivated to feed.

I paused as a song sparrow perched on a raspberry bush to clean herself. She quietly chirped as she reached down with her beak to meticulously preen each fluffed-up feather. She belonged on this patch of ground; she looked fat and sassy, claiming that bush as her territory. As I continued to walk, the insect life erupted with every step. Bees collected nectar on the still-blooming aster, and beetles crawled across the path that lay before me. The life in this small three-quarter-acre yard felt boundless. There was more life and diversity in this three-quarter-acre patch than any three-quarter-acre area on the National Seashore we'd just left, which the government had deemed a wildlife refuge and where signs told people to leave only footprints and take only pictures.

The food forest that lay around me had many of the elements I had witnessed in the ecologically intact wilderness areas I had tracked where natural predators and prey still thrived, such as Alaska, Idaho, and some parts of Washington. This place was different, however, and gave me a sense of permanence beyond measure. Everywhere I looked I saw recognizable food plants and animals for meat and eggs. The perennial plants, the fruit and nut trees, and the animals that foraged were a direct result of the intentional design Penny and her husband James had propagated on this place. The animals were the only source of fertilizer; no external inputs were necessary.

Beyond the wall of multistory plants lay functional and aesthetically pleasing dwellings. A cob library made from clay, sand, and straw sat at one end of the garden next to the koi and duck pond. On the side of the dwelling, a sculpted dragon with an open mouth shaped the bench and outdoor pizza oven. Edging the roof was a flexible pipe that captured the rainwater from the roof, which was then directed toward the pond to be stored. The surface of the pond reflected the low sun of late fall and winter up to the windows of the dwelling to brighten and warm the inside of the cob office. Every element had an intentional place within the design, taking into consideration sun, wind, water flow, and potential natural disasters such as fire and flood.

Toward the back of the garden sat a vaulted straw bale dwelling. This is where I was to stay for the night. As I entered the dwelling, which looked more like a hobbit hole than a house, I was overwhelmed with the sensations of the place. Bamboo supported the inside structure and the bales of straw were covered in a lightly pigmented earthen plaster. I could see plants, chickens, ducks, and wildlife from my window. The room was just big enough for a bed, a small desk, and a nightstand, and the inside spaces served only the basic needs of shelter, food storage, and cooking—a cozy place that nevertheless encouraged me to look outside, to go outside.

As my friendship with Penny grew, I joined up with her project, the Regenerative Design Institute, and began taking every permaculture course she and her colleagues led. I continued to live at the field station in the Santa Cruz Mountains part-time. Now at twenty-one years old, I split my time between my job as a tracker and my training in permaculture. I spent half of every week with Penny for a year, teaching nature awareness to her students in exchange for her mentoring me in permaculture. I was a giant sponge in the presence of permaculture teachers. What I learned I directly applied at my own home at the field station and with the people and places I visited.

As the sky turned dark that first night I visited Penny, and I could no longer see the new discoveries I was making in this backyard paradise, I adjourned inside where Penny and her family were busily preparing a meal. Baskets of eggs, basil, and perennial kale sat out on the counter, the harvest from out the back steps. A jar was pulled from the shelf of the tomato harvest earlier in the season, steaks bought from a nearby cattle rancher baked in the oven, and black dirt was scrubbed from the potatoes. As we sat and shared the meal prepared from the land, we laughed and shared stories. The love that was present not only for the people around the table but of the life outside the door was as perennial as the native bunchgrasses we had earlier discovered. That patch of grass on the National Seashore would continue to hold on, despite the alien species that dominated their expansive prairie and the lack of people tending the wild in the park. The following year, Penny would go and collect those seeds and spread that infinite perennial love.

Easy ways to start eating like a regenetarian

PUT YOUR ROOTS IN THE GROUND

The first step to starting a garden is to build soil, even just a small patch in your backyard. You can compost your kitchen scraps and yard waste to add more carbon to the soil. This not only builds the health of the soil and keeps the soil moist but also helps to draw down carbon. Then start a garden, even a few plants in your windowsill or yard. Grow something from seed to harvest. You could start with some perennial herbs like rosemary or sage that will grow for many years. Visit a garden store or look for seed catalogues and plant something that you really like to eat. One of my favorites is a sun choke, also known as a Jerusalem artichoke. It is a species native to North America, but will grow in many climates. It is a tuber, like a potato, that is planted in the ground once and produces a beautiful sunflower every year. It will keep giving food for many years with very little work.

PICK UP SOME CHICKS

When I was growing up I spent a lot of time with chickens. They are the ultimate role model. They wake up early, get to work pecking and scratching, and lay an egg a day. Plus you can save your kitchen scraps like veggies and grains and they will happily eat them. You can get a few baby chicks from a catalogue or feed store along with a heat lamp to keep them warm for the first month of their life. Once they have fledged (gotten their feathers) they can go outside. They need a small shelter where they can be protected from predators and ideally some grass where they can peck around and eat bugs and seeds. Chickens have personalities, and they can quickly become part of the family. They certainly earn their keep when you taste their eggs—they are so much better than anything you can get in a supermarket!

GET TO KNOW YOUR LOCAL FARMERS

Who is your closest farmer? The best way to find your farmers is to visit your local farmers' market. You can find out who is growing diversified vegetables, grass-fed meats, and organic fruits. Make a map of all the farms in your region and what they grow. Start to ask if you can visit those farms. Are they open to the public or do they offer tours? You can then adventure to see the source of your food. Ask questions about what farmers grow and how they grow it. Find out if they care for the soil and why the soil is important to the food they produce. Once you have that map of the foodshed, the geographic location of where your food comes from and where it travels, then challenge yourself to eat as locally as possible, where you know the source of your food.

VOLUNTEER ON A FARM

When I was a teenager I would do some work in exchange
for a box of veggies at our local organic CSA farm. I loved
the work. I would weed, plant seeds in flats in the greenhouse
listening to loud Bob Marley music, harvest lettuce and car-
rots, and enjoy getting my hands dirty. I got to become friends
with the farmers, be outside, and learn a ton. My family
would also glean at farms like our local basil farm and apple
orchards. To glean means to go into the field after the farmer
has harvested the crop and find and pick what is left behind.
Often they will leave the bases of the plants, such as basil, and
only take the tops because they will sell better. There is often
still a lot of food out in the fields or fruit on the trees after
the farmer has harvested. Sometimes the fruits are blemished,
but they are still delicious. If we gleaned large amounts we
would then preserve the food for winter. After I would go to
the basil farm with my family, we would go home and make
pesto, freeze it, and have it through the winter. We got outside,
got our exercise, and saved money, all while using what would
have been wasted.

Home

When I first laid eyes on him, and not just his tracks, I was stumbling through the front door of the field station after a long morning out tracking and checking my camera line. I was a mess. I had crawled through a thicket of coastal scrub tracking a grey fox, an animal much smaller than I and able to maneuver in tight spaces. My pants were covered in dirt, I was wearing an old ratty tank top, and my bare arms revealed scratches from the hard branches of ironwood and poison oak. The smell of my sweat hung in the air around me. Then I looked up, and there he was.

My heart started racing. He reached out his hand to shake mine. Stumbling over my words, I looked into his bright green eyes. They pierced me as if I were a clear lake and he could see to my depths.

The Riekes field station where I lived and worked was always bustling with people. Visiting trackers and authors, friends, and family were always welcomed and offered a bed.

Some never left. As my fellow tracking friends began mingling, I took a look at the stranger in the house from the corner of the room. He wore ripped jeans, scuffed cowboy boots, a T-shirt, and a dirty black cowboy hat with a red-tailed hawk feather poking out of the horsehair hatband. I noticed his hands—large and calloused. He looked as if every muscle in his body was toned for practical reasons. His skin was tough to the elements. I could tell by looking at him that he had spent most of his life outside in pursuit of physical labor.

He walked over to a large poster on the wall. I angled across the room toward him. Quickly running my fingers through my dirty blond hair, which held more dirt than blond, I attempted to look less disheveled. He squinted at the topographical map on the wall, then slowly looked at the map key showing colored dots with the names of animal species next to them.

"Grey fox, bobcat, coyote, mountain lion, deer, raccoon, skunk…" he read aloud in a baritone voice, then turned and pierced my eyes with his again. "Those points are all over Broken Arrow Ranch," he stated angrily. "How could you have been out there tracking this whole time without me seeing you?"

My heart was practically beating out of my chest; I thought this was the end of our fleeting interaction. We'd never even met before—I had only heard the neighbors talk of his position as rock star Neil Young's ranch manager. Had I jeopardized his job by trespassing all over the land that he was meant to keep secure, safe from intruders who could harm his animals or carelessly set fire to the grasslands? He kept the ranch, about two thousand acres in size according to the neighbors, secure for his boss, who had a fan base known to travel from across the world to attempt to camp on the rock star's ranch and get a glimpse of Neil. Had I disrespected a boundary or code of ranchers—*you keep to your land and I keep to mine?* Just when the silent tension between us had built to unbearable levels, the side of his mouth rose up in a half smile. He got a mischievous look in those green eyes.

The week before, Tiffany, a fellow tracker who was also living and working out of the field station in the Santa Cruz Mountains, walked in the door from one of her long treks alone. She was a serious student of tracking. Blond, with a slight build, she was transitioning from being a professional skateboarder and running an all-girls skate company to wildlife tracking. She had grabbed a glass of water, thrown down her backpack, and collapsed on the couch.

"I got caught trespassing," she said as she threw her head back against the couch.

I pulled up a chair next to the couch and asked her what happened.

Tiffany responded, "I was tracking upstream, past the steelhead spawning ground and over the big log jam. I decided to go up the steep bank of the creek to see if I could pick up the tracks of the male mountain lion. I had seen his tracks along the bank of the creek veer off up the hill. I used the switch-backing animal trails so I could find the trail paralleling the creek up toward the ridge."

I could picture the place, and I knew it was rough going. The creek was in a deep gorge with steep banks on either side. In some places the only way through was to wade in deep water or jump from rock to rock, being careful not to slip on the slick surface.

"I came to a large pasture edged with redwood forest and got disoriented. There was a knob with a cattle fence that cut across the center. Have you been up there?" I nodded my head. I had trespassed there a time or two myself in pursuit of the mountain lion. She continued. "I wasn't thinking and I went out into the open to this high grassy knob."

Tiffany walked over to the kitchen to refill her glass of water. Curious about how she got caught, I waited patiently for her to come back to the couch to continue. "I was barely on top of that knob for like a minute. It was so pretty up there, with those big redwood trees going right up to the edge of the grass. Then I got caught out in the open like a dummy. Some guy on a four-wheeler was racing toward me. I looked to the edge of the forests and then looked back at the dude. I didn't know what to do, so I ran at first but I knew it was no use. So I surrendered. The four-wheeler stopped right next to me and sitting on top of it was a tall guy in a black cowboy hat." Slouching down in the couch even more, she seemed as though she wanted to disappear. She was trained in stealth, how to move without detection, and she had made the rookie mistake of getting caught out in the open. "Then he started asking me a bunch of questions like, What was I doing there? Where did I live? So I told him where I lived. The guy knew exactly where it was and named all the people who lived here before us. It was like he was trying to make a point that he not only kept tabs on his ranch but of all the neighbors too. He named all these people I've never heard of, like he was pointing out that he had grown up in the area and lived here a lot longer than me. Like I really cared," she said sarcastically. "So I told him I was lost, even though I knew that I could just go back down to the creek and follow it back. But then he said, 'You can fool the fans but not the players.' He didn't believe that I could be lost when I was living on forty acres and had traveled over three miles away to end up in the middle of his two-thousand-acre cattle ranch."

We typically kept our work quiet because we did not want to spur any heated discussions about large predators near livestock—I'd learned this lesson the world over, that many people are scared of and/or angry at predators. And most people don't know what to think about someone walking through the woods following the footprints of an animal.

"When he kept interrogating me I finally told him I was tracking mountain lions and their territory encompassed this watershed and I had to travel through his ranch because mountain lions cover a lot of ground and aren't easy to track. Then his demeanor totally changed from interrogation to intrigue. And I realized this was my golden ticket to freedom. He said, 'So you had to stretch the fence of your forty-acre property? I guess I can see that.' I continued with the mountain lion talk and then told him about you and how you had set up cameras along the banks of the creek and the old logging roads and had gotten pictures of them."

I wasn't so happy she'd involved me in her bailout.

"So he said he wanted to see those pictures and meet the person who got them. He said he loved mountain lions but had never seen one in the wild, even though he had lived his whole life exploring that creek. He camped on it as a kid and set up swings and cliff jumps into the deep pools."

Imitating his manly voice, Tiffany continued with a scowl. "Then he said to me, 'Do you have a pen and paper in that backpack? I want your phone number.' He was looking at my sagging pack slung over my shoulders and I tried to avoid the conversation and told him I just had a water bottle, but he didn't believe me. Then he reached in his pocket and took out his knife. I kinda got freaked out, but he walked over to his four-wheeler, he grabbed the plastic fender, and stuck the point of the knife to the plastic. He said 'I'm ready for your number.' So I told him the number and he scratched it into the fender with his knife. Then he pointed to the most direct route back to the field station, lifted one leg over the machine as if it were a horse, and rode off over the rolling hills the way he had come."

Just then the phone rang. I jumped up to grab it.

"Hello, my name is Erik Markegard," the voice on the line said. "I live on the ranch next door and I just met someone who said they have a friend with pictures of the mountain lions in my creek. I would like to come and see those pictures. I can come right now and be there in ten minutes," he continued in a polite tone of voice.

Holding the phone away from my ear and covering the mouthpiece, I whispered to Tiffany, "It's the guy who just caught you trespassing." She shrugged her shoulders and walked over to lean into the conversation. Taking my hand away from the plastic phone, I replied slowly, "I'm the one who has pictures of the mountain lions in Corte de Madera Creek. I can give you a call later; today is not a good day."

After a few minutes of Erik attempting to break my reluctance to invite him over immediately, he gave me his number and got off the phone.

I turned to Tiffany and said, "I think I tracked that dude up above Gary's cabin."

A couple months earlier, while I was checking the cameras I had set out to capture images of mountain lions, I had seen large boot tracks in the soft layer of leaves below the ceanothus trees filled with sweet-smelling blue flowers. The film had run out, so I didn't get a picture of the intruder. Reaching my hand down to touch the tracks, I ran my fingertips along the edge without moving the debris. I felt a heel on the boot, the size of a work boot, and a large track—men's size eleven or twelve. I crouched and peered down the trail. He had a long stride with toes pointing out. And on a different occasion, I'd heard a vehicle approaching rapidly on the neighboring ranch where Tiffany was caught. I jumped behind a large bush just to the side of the trail. I peered through the branches from my hiding spot as a man with a black cowboy hat sped by riding a green four-wheeler, trailed by a black-and-white dog.

During the awkward moment when Erik first came down to meet me, the person who had captured the pictures of mountain lions in "his" creek, I saw him walk over with a long stride, feet splayed out. I knew it was him I'd tracked. When I saw the sparkle in his eyes as he looked at me on that first meeting, I realized I hadn't botched it with Erik by letting him see I'd been all over his ranch, tracking undetected.

In that first meeting I caught on to his teasing demeanor and played along, saying, "It was not only animals I tracked in 'your' creek."

"I want you to teach me how to track," he responded, as if I had no choice in the matter.

A lifelong friendship began that day between wildlife tracker and cattle rancher.

Erik spent as much time with me as possible whenever I was at the field station and not Penny's. He would call early in the mornings to see if I was headed out tracking and always seemed to show up just as I was finishing cooking up a hot chicken soup or a making a cup of tea. Often he brought the person he called the love of his life. He always carried her picture in his wallet and proudly showed everyone her photo. I noticed right away he was an amazing father and his beautiful little girl, Lea, meant the world to him.

The field station was only a five-minute four-wheeler ride from Erik's house. A barbed-wire fence separated the two properties—the forty acres where I lived and the two-thousand-acre ranch where he was born and raised. After parking his four-wheeler on his side of the fence, he would climb on a rotten stump and push down the top of the fence to walk down the steep driveway to my house. The stump soon became worn with his trail, collapsing with consistent use. He never came empty-handed: he always brought gifts of fresh eggs from his chickens, beef from his freezer, or fish a local fisher buddy had given him.

Getting to know a rancher was new for me. The only experience I had around cattle and ranching was in the Interior West, where I had spent my summers tracking wolves in the Frank Church–River of No Return Wilderness. When I drove to the edge of that wilderness and saw land degraded by overgrazing, I developed a murky opinion of ranchers. It took me some time to see Erik as something different from those other ranchers, the ones I'd been warned not to talk to about my work, the ones I could never tell the whereabouts of the wolves to, since, according to the biologists, the ranchers in that area wanted nothing more than to shoot any wolf they came across.

I grew to see Erik as a different sort of rancher, one who genuinely loved and cared about all of the natural world, and what I observed within the grasslands on Erik's ranches held a solution for humans becoming regenetarians. Many grasslands, which cover as much as 40 percent of the earth's surface area, are doomed for extinction. Large grasslands have been destroyed and converted into agricultural cropland. This shrinks the diversity from hundreds of species found in an intact grassland, providing habitat and carbon and water storage along with watershed protection to many major river systems, down to just a handful of food and fodder species grown on these same lands and not providing those ecosystem services (Panunzi 2008). I could see that a design as intentional as the three-quarter-acre backyard of Penny's needed to be spread across the grasslands, and it had to include livestock and ranchers as stewards of the land and animals.

The term for this intentional design of grasslands is Holistic Management, a method based on the principle that nature functions in wholes and no one part can be isolated or changed without impacting the whole. It is a system of management that states that in order to make effective decisions that are socially, environmentally, and economically sound, one must learn to understand nature and then apply appropriate tools to get at the root cause of problems. Managing livestock by mimicking the predator-prey relationships to create the disturbances with which these grasslands evolved is one tool Holistic Management uses (Savory 1999). Ranchers who have a keen eye for regeneration, grassland, and animal health are able to be ecological stewards of land, water, soil, and animals, and still make a living.

When I moved beyond my prejudice that all ranchers were bad and looked purely at what was in front of me, without bringing my stories from the past into the present moment, I saw something unique. Erik and the land he stewarded actually held an abundance of life, unlike the depleted agriculture crop fields I'd experienced before. When I had hopped the fence over to the cattle pasture to track animals on the ranch surrounding the field station where I lived and worked, I noticed a distinct difference between the vibrancy of the life in the areas that the cattle had grazed and the side of the fence where I was living, where cattle had not grazed for fifteen years. It was similar to what I'd experienced going from the parkland to Penny's garden.

On our side of the fence, it was like the biological cycles of life had hit the pause button and there was no longer a reason for the species to thrive. These grasses on the field station side lacked diversity and were bent over, hiding bare ground below. In the cycle of a grass plant—birth, growth, death, and decay, repeated infinitely—the plant had been robbed of decay, and so the whole cycle had stopped. The decay was simply not present on my side of the fence. The very life-giving process that I had experienced in the wet forests of my homeland, in which decay fed the entire web of life, was nearly nonexistent where the cattle had been removed. Here in California there was a lot less rain than in Western Washington, just about half, and only in a few months out of the year rather than spread throughout the twelve months. Without the presence of rain, what kept the decay part of the cycle going? On Erik's side of the fence, it was thriving.

This realization led to my learning about what Holistic Management calls the *brittleness scale*. The range of the scale is based on the distribution of humidity throughout the year. On the non-brittle side of the scale are the rainforests, similar to where I grew up in Western Washington, where rainfall and humidity are scattered throughout the year and dead vegetation breaks down rapidly. On the opposite end of the brittleness scale would be very brittle, or desert. The vegetation in brittle environments, such as the tall standing grass on my side of the fence in summer, can easily be snapped when bent by hand. In California, with seasonal rainfall, we were closer to the brittle side, and there needed to be living organisms present in order to stimulate the breakdown of vegetation.

On the working cattle ranch side of the fence, I entered a tracker's paradise. Vole trails wove in and out of the grass. The grasses and herbaceous plants stood only five or six inches from the ground as opposed to a few feet on my side of the fence. The plants were vibrant green here; the field station side was brown. Flipping over a cow pie, I found the decay I'd been looking for. White strands of mycelium spread out across the overturned brown saucer along with beetles, ants, and pill bugs. Each disc of manure was surrounded by vibrant green grass, a conspicuous contradiction of green and greener.

The grasses, fungi, and insects were not the only ones reaping the benefits of decay. There were a myriad of predators both on the ground and in flight taking full advantage of the open hunting ground, due to grasses that were only about six inches high, that left the larder of the vole more exposed and vulnerable than on my side of the fence where the grasses were a few feet tall and bent over. This cycle was powered by the sun shining down onto the green leaves of the grass plants, inducing a photosynthetic lure that all life was nourished by.

And the only difference from one side of the pasture to the other was the presence of the herd of herbivores. This is the key element in brittle environments, where at times rain only falls for a few months out of the year: herbivores promote the decaying cycle through disturbance and excrement. In non-brittle environments, such as the tropical rainforests, the microbes that aid decay are found in the top layers of the soil. In brittle environments, those beneficial microbes live in the gut of a herd of grazing hoofed mammals, eventually making their way out through feces to then feed the soil.

Erik called early one warm spring morning as I was sitting drinking tea looking out the window at the spotted towhee scratching with both feet backing up at the same time to disturb the surface of the ground, then reaching its beak down to feast on the unsuspecting seeds and insects. I was engrossed in the bird and very disturbed by the interrupting ring. He told me that his friend Herbie had been riding dirt bikes in the back of Toto Ranch and had seen a mountain lion. Toto Ranch was the coastal ranch Erik leased for his own cattle operation, the ranch where he was typically found after work or on weekends wrenching on trucks, building fence, or riding his own dirt bike or horse.

"Herbie saw the mountain lion cross the trail in front of him!" Erik was so excited he could hardly contain himself. He asked if I could come look for tracks. I had hoped to go surfing that morning, as there was a nice offshore breeze and the swell was really good now that the winter storms had passed, but he would not take no for an answer.

When I finally agreed to meet him on Toto Ranch, he exclaimed that he would be there in twenty minutes and hung up the phone. Tiffany and her twin sister, Nicole (the fellow tracker who had gotten lost with me in Idaho on the trail of a wolf), and I loaded up some surfboards on the roof of my car and headed out the door wearing shorts and sandals. When we arrived at the front gate of the ranch with a wooden archway over the top that read TOTO, Erik was there to greet us. He drove a big lifted Ford diesel truck with mud tires that dwarfed the little diesel Volkswagen I drove. I had converted my car to run on waste vegetable oil I collected from restaurants and was put off by his diesel-guzzling machine.

We drove up the mile-long driveway, with views of the ragged cliffs of Tunitas Creek Beach as the backdrop. The ranch was a grassland paradise. As we drove, a group of white-tailed kites hovered over the open grass, awaiting the right moment to drop straight down upon the critters below. A red-tailed hawk perched on the fence post and took off in flight as our car approached, displaying the underside of its wings striped in browns and whites. We parked next to the old yellow ranch house. We then headed out toward the back of the ranch, away from the ocean.

Walking slowly and stopping occasionally to take a look around, we experienced the place through all our senses. We were observing the land to look for trails the animals may frequent and studying the food and water sources for wildlife— just a few things we did as trackers when we first arrived at a new place. This place was like candy for the senses. The sweet smell and taste of the coastal salt air combined with the sight of green rolling hills undulating up from the expanse of ocean sparked a feeling of freedom, aliveness, and possibility.

We stopped on the ridge above the house and looked out to the south. I heard the alarms of song sparrows in the coyote brush. One had risen to the top of the highest bush, and with its beak angled toward the ground, it sounded a harsh chip repeated in a rhythmic pattern. I pointed to a coyote who had spooked and was running away from us. Tiffany, Nicole, and I kept our talking to an infrequent whisper, but Erik could not contain his excitement. I was used to being silent in nature, keeping small talk to a minimum so I could be fully aware of what was going on around me. Erik, on the other hand, despite what I had taught him so far about tracking, was proud as a peacock to showcase the ranch that he had taken on when he was eighteen years old, fresh out of high school, as his own project with his own cattle. His classmates all went on to study for careers in business and the trades; Erik was the only one in the rural high school class who pursued his passion and lineage in ranching.

Pointing to a stock pond, he explained that he had built it to capture the water from springs and rainwater flowing over the land. He boasted that he built twelve of them one summer with a D6 CAT and an excavator. Dug in prominent places in the landscape where water collected at high points, the ponds captured the water. If he hadn't created the catchments, the water would still be running off, picking up sediment and therefore nutrients within the soil as it gained velocity across the hills. The hills of the ranch still held the scars of erosion from the time before Erik built the stock ponds, before he managed to keep the ground covered the entire year with green growing plants. Historic farming and ranching had not kept the water cycling in the grassland plants; instead the water washed over the land, creating the scars in the form of erosion gullies. We passed by one area where a series of ponds linked together, each overflowing into the next. The ponds flowed like the masterfully engineered beaver wonderlands I grew up around in Washington State. I had not seen beaver in this part of California; they had been hunted during the fur rush of the eighteen hundreds nearly to their demise.

While we were walking along the edge of the pond, a red-legged frog jumped out of a little pool of water collected in the hoofprint of a cow. I jumped too, with excitement, as this was the first time I had seen this endangered species. Erik explained that when he first came to the ranch there was not enough water for his herd of cattle, so he'd built these ponds. The following spring the frogs had appeared in large numbers and their chorus was deafening. Along with the frogs moving in, the canvasback, bufflehead, hooded merganser, and other ducks found a favorite spot to land on their migratory flight, where there was none before. The unintentional outcome of an overly energized eighteen-year-old riding on a big yellow machine while developing the ranch of his dreams was this: a home in a hoofprint for the endangered red-legged frog and solace for a duck on a long journey.

Erik's personality and work ethic were contagious. I was inspired by the idea that if one young individual could create a frog oasis on one thousand acres, then there was hope for these endangered frog species, which played a vital role in maintaining the balance of wetland ecosystems. Their tadpoles fed on algae, keeping the water clean, and the frogs fed on insects, reducing fly and mosquito populations. In all stages of their life, frogs are food to an array of predators such as birds, fish, snakes, raccoons, and even coyotes. Nearly one-third of amphibians are threatened with extinction (IUCN, Conservation International, and NatureServe 2004). Counter to my image of ranchers destroying the environment, the work of this one lone rancher was beyond what any pencil-pushing environmentalist I knew had achieved.

As we wrapped around to a hill overlooking the stunning views of a vast blue ocean with silver specks that reflected the sun like precious gems, we came across a large patch of stinging nettle. Erik motioned for us to stop. He turned to the three of us and pointed out the plant. "Don't touch that, it will sting you," he said with authority. He looked in dismay at our bare legs and glanced at his worn Wrangler jeans, then continued. "You won't want to brush your legs against that stinging nettle or you'll feel it for a long time."

As he went on to warn us of the dangers of nature, being our protector out in the bush, I leaned over the plant to study it, looking as if I was really taking his advice seriously. Reaching down with my fingertips, with an upward motion I pulled the top part of the plant off. The hairs of the stinging nettle plant face upwards toward the sun; when harvested, if the fine hairs are stroked in an upward motion, like stroking a horse in the direction the hair grows, the plant will not sting. Once I had the top of the plant in my hand, I folded the leaves in on each other carefully, making sure I was going in the same direction as the hairs. I crumpled it up until the vibrant green ball was moist with plant juices. I popped it in my mouth and started chewing. Erik stood in silence, staring at me in astonishment.

We did not find the mountain lion that day. But after seeing Erik in his element, and the way that he carefully tended his land, I found myself falling in love.

Erik and I continued our search for mountain lions in the following months. Just before the day at Toto Ranch, we had set up a camera on an old logging road on Broken Arrow Ranch, up the creek from the Riekes field station. We had found several areas along that road where mountain lions had scratched the duff in the road. We speculated the marks were left by a male, as they tend to scrape more often to communicate dominance, leaving a scent mark from their interdigital glands as a calling card for other wildlife. We decided there was a good chance we would capture an image. The redwood debris that had fallen from the trees was scraped into a small neat pile, which the mountain lion does with their hind feet, one foot after the other in a parallel fashion, leaving a territorial visual and scent mark (Elbroch and Rinehart 2011). When we found the scrape marks on the road, Erik glanced over at me excitedly, like a little kid waiting in line for a roller coaster. Mountain lions permeated his thoughts throughout the day and his dreams at night the way wolves had mine. He always had a love for the large felids, and since he'd learned to recognize their tracks and signs he was constantly on the lookout for scrapes on the ground, shiny firm scats larger than an inch diameter with a pungent smell, tracks around watering holes, and scratches on downed logs.

I explained to Erik that we could be waiting a long time for this mountain lion to return. Wandering through large expanses is fundamental to the life of a mountain lion. Even if there is abundant prey in one area, like where we set the camera, they may still wander far, maybe even twenty miles in one night, to return at some unknown time in the future, possibly not for months. With the camera set, we waited patiently for the film to run out so we could send it off for development. At that point there were no motion-sensing cameras available with digital images, so we had to wait.

After months of checking the camera that was set on the logging roads of Broken Arrow Ranch, developing film to find intriguing pictures of the grey fox carrying a brush rabbit in its mouth on the way to a den, a brave bobcat marking the mountain lion scrape in the redwood duff where we placed the camera, and a doe with her two fawns walking cautiously, we had not captured the elusive mountain lion.

But then one day, I went to pick up the next set of pictures at the store, and I flipped through them while standing in the checkout line. There he was. My hands shook and I started to sweat. I was gazing at a large wounded male mountain lion who had walked through the infrared beam. The picture was absolutely magnificent. Staring at a large wet gash across his hip, I could picture that cat lying in its day bed licking the wound as I had seen house cats do. Possibly the wound was from a hunt or a fight with another male mountain lion over territory.

The mountain lions hunt with precision, lying in wait or stalking low to the ground with ears perked until they are within striking range of their prey. When they make their explosive chase and pounce, they hold on with their sharp, retractable claws, the claws that are protected while traveling, only to come out when their survival depends on it like swords being drawn from a sheath. With four claws in the front and a fifth larger claw hidden up higher on the cat's wrist, they hold on while their prey runs and bucks like a bronc in a rodeo doing anything to throw off the rider. Possibly the gash on this mountain lion I was looking at in the photo could have been an antler strike from a buck before the cat was able to sink its stiletto-like canines, which have nerves running to the tips of the teeth for them to feel when they have worked their way between the vertebrae, for the quick killing bite into the back of the neck or skull of their prey (Elbroch and Rienhart 2011).

I wanted to know that animal. I wanted to know where it went and how it traveled. I wanted to feel humbled in the presence of a creature so massive and powerful that the jaws could break though large bones and take a deer down with a killing bite of the spinal cord. This mountain lion demanded my respect, helped me to remember to be aware and that humans are not the top predator, but we are merely a member of the group of animals who have the instincts to hunt for sustenance.

Mountain lions, a keystone species, communicate so much

about the movement and patterns of all the other species they interact with. The prey species' behavior changes if a mountain lion is around; prey becomes less likely to be seen out in the open and moves more frequently, never loafing in an area too long. The other predators, such as the bobcat, fox, and coyote, change their hunting patterns and are seen more in the day because the mountain lion dominates the nights and the time when dark and light merge.

A few months later, we got another picture of the mountain lion at that same camera site, and a half hour later the same mountain lion passed through a different camera site that was set up with an active beam that worked like a trip line. We were starting to get an idea of this animal's movement patterns, predicting where it would travel based on the tracks we found, then setting up a string of cameras to see if we could get multiple pictures of the same animal, traveling long distances in the protection of cover, remaining undetected by most humans, in pursuit of prey and a mate. Pure passion fueled the dirt time of crawling down animal trails, searching for carcasses of deer killed by mountain lions, mapping the entire watershed to predict the most likely travel routes based on cover, food source, and trail choice. I found they traveled on trails unobstructed by brush, often paralleling the steep creek drainages, just on the down slope side of the ridge. Following these trails drove me to wake up an hour before first light to be out on the trail before the chirp of the American robins as they rustled in their roosts.

I tracked voraciously, often with Erik. We drank from clean

springs bubbling out of the ground in the immense redwood forests and nibbled on the wild edibles that grew in and on the edges of the forest. The redwood sorrel, the chickweed and miner's lettuce kept our energy up if we had forgotten to stuff a snack in our pockets.

Mountain lions led me to Erik; or rather, they led Erik to me. We had been living in parallel territories, circling each other in our respective home ranges, like mountain lions, leaving our mark on the earth until we would unite and together leave our mark for the future.

One day, as Erik and I were taking a rest in a pasture after having tracked since the early morning, I asked him about his cattle and the way they roamed. He explained to me that his father, Larry, had observed that the pastures needed to rest and have time when cattle were not grazing them. That gave the grasses a chance to grow and the manure a chance to decompose. The flies and other parasites were able to continue out their cycle without bothering the cattle, and the cattle followed their natural instincts as herd animals moving through the range. Erik and his father, who had never been introduced to Holistic Management and the methods that Allan Savory laid out in his work, had come to this philosophy of grassland stewardship purely through observing and interacting with their landscape.

Learning from his father, Erik on horseback moved his

cattle from one fenced-in pasture to the next. As he went
to open a gate into a new pasture for the cattle, he gave out
a loud call. "Oh Vye," he bellowed with a long, drawn-out
voice. He called and the cattle knew that the sound meant
they would move from the pasture where they had just
grazed, urinated, defecated, and trampled into a new, untainted pasture. The herd moving across the land caused enough
of a disturbance in the soil for seeds to find their way into
the pockmarks of the cattle hoofprints, which also collected
water. Still on his horse, he then moved to the back of the
group, gathering up any of the stragglers that did not take the
hint from the rest of the herd that it was time to move on to,
literally, greener pastures.

Carefully eyeing each animal in the herd of 250, he looked
for any sign of weakness or illness. Erik had a sharp look in his
eye and an attentive demeanor about him when he observed
his land and livestock, picking up on the subtle cues from the
herd. He looked at a pregnant cow moving slowly at the back
of the herd, indicating she may be close to giving birth. He
noticed a steer with a collection of flies around him, showing
early signs of weakness. His gut feeling guided him to an animal needing a closer look. He had a keen sense of the grasses,
the weather, and the patterns of rainfall, as well. He worked
with a mixture of intuition and common sense. He made his
living caring for his cattle in a way a parent cares for a child,
and he knew that his animals could only be as healthy as the
grasslands they grazed on.

Broken Arrow, Neil Young's ranch, where Erik was born and raised, was located in the Corte de Madera watershed, the same creek basin where I lived at the field station. The large creek that rippled over boulders and through redwood groves bubbled out from a pile of rocks and debris up the hill from Erik's house. Deer Fork, one of the sources of the creek, supported houses, ranches, and farms as well as all the species of wildlife who made their home within the watershed. As the creek wove its way through the forest in the deep canyon, small tributaries fed the main stem of the creek, forming branching patterns. This watershed was what one of my permaculture mentors, Brock Dolman, would call our "basin of relation." Everything we did within the watershed affected all who lived within it.

The watershed was our lifeboat. From the ridgeline to the river mouth or the summit to the sea, our dependency on pure, clean water to drink and grow our food was held within the decisions of those living within the watershed. The care of the soils and the grasslands impacted the pureness of the water that was shed, being captured amongst the plants, in the piping of houses, and in reservoirs. All the uses of the water as it traveled from source to sink made up the fate of both the life in the creek, such as the salmon, and the life in the ocean just a few miles away.

Agribusinesses across the United States don't typically think in terms of watershed. The dead zone the size of Texas at the mouth of the Mississippi is a prime example of the corn and soy agribusinesses only looking at property boundaries and extracting the most they can out of their plot of land. Soil is the largest export in our country, thoughtlessly removed from where it was built up for millions of years only to end up washed out through streams and rivers or blown away to go airborne. The agricultural sector is the world's second largest emitter of greenhouse gases after the energy sector, and carbon emissions in agriculture grew 14 percent from 2001 to 2011. The obvious solution is to draw that hovering carbon down into the soil (Russell 2014; FAO 2014).

The solution had been sitting in front of me this entire time. It took the cattle to show me. Herbivores enhance the cycling of nutrients, in turn creating thriving grass plants which, through photosynthesis, sequester atmospheric carbon (Bellows 2001). An overgrazed expanse of grassland—or an abandoned crop field that at one point was a grassland—could, with intentional planning and management to accomplish land health, human well-being, and financial prosperity, be shifted into a carbon sink. If land has a capped surface, a hard surface that stops water from penetrating, very little will grow there. Capping of soil happens when land is rested and does not have grazing herds providing disturbance and fertility. This capped, bare soil, eroded by wind, sun, and rain, could be broken up by animal hooves, creating contact between the dormant seeds and the soil. Those animals could apply fertilizer out their hind ends, too. Then grasses return, which means more cattle can be grazed.

Ranchers can put up solar electric fencing to keep cattle bunched up, giving the grasses time to recover, mimicking wild herds, which would have stayed close together for protection from predators. They can also move them frequently, as a wild herd has to do when predators are nearby. This results in more plants, deeper roots, and larger swathes of growing vegetation to pull the carbon into the soil. Photosynthesis, keeping the ground covered, and enhancing the carbon cycle all generate nutrient-rich humus, the dark brown decaying organic matter, which will eventually turn into soil, that stores water at the capacity of one part humus to four parts water (Wheeler and Ward 2006).

I had struck the harmonic chord in my search. With human creativity of design, which included using living organisms as the master regenerators, I had arrived at the complete answer to the question I'd posed that night at Cedar Falls at seventeen years old, when I stepped out of the wilderness determined to be part of the regeneration of a degraded planet. I already knew that I needed to help heal the planet; I knew that food would be part of my work. Now I knew that I could, through ranching with Holistic Management, be part of an agriculture practice that—instead of being an emitter of greenhouse gases—would work with nature to draw down carbon and be part of the solution to the climate crises (O'Mara 2012; Teague et al. 2016).

Erik proposed to me on a hill he named Joint Point, which had 360-degree views of the entire watershed and the ocean. At sunset, with his blue merle Australian shepherd dog Kiowa as our witness, we sat together embracing as the sun slowly sank and colors marked the celebration of the transition of day and night and a new life of two souls becoming bonded together as one. I had remembered what he said about family and saw how he loved and cared for his daughter. He said that caring for his family meant everything to him. He lived for the love and closeness of family. I had never met anyone so dedicated and focused on that one outcome. I had always had big visions of the planet and a change for humanity. There was a simplicity of the importance of providing for your family that opened up my heart to his, and I knew he was the one I would continue this journey with. My inclination was always to look outward to find meaning in the work I did. Now it was time to move inward and care for home like a humming-bird building a nest, choosing every soft item from lichen to spider webs to build a beautiful work of art in which to raise her young. Erik would embody the second principle, *Wo-cante' k*na-ke*, to have love and compassion for those close to you. He would love and care for his children, and they would mean the world to him. I thought that if every father were as loving and caring as Erik, that action alone would save the earth and humanity from the crisis of hatred. I wanted my children to have a father who made keeping the home fire burning his number one priority.

Erik and I made our life commitments to each other in a Lakota wedding ceremony conducted by Gilbert Walking Bull. As he led the ceremony, all of the lines of wrinkles in my adoptive father's dark round face were jovial. Gilbert had a guttural chortle that made his whole body shake. Others could not help but smile and laugh along joyously. When he spoke, everyone listened. Each word that came out was a deliberate message for all present to hear. Erik and I stood there on Tunitas Beach that fall day, our hands tied together with a red cloth and a star quilt my mother had made wrapped around both of us. We committed to finding the quiet peace within ourselves. We committed to health of mind, body, and spirit. We committed to happiness, curiosity, and awe. We committed to the growth and abundance of all creation. Lastly, we committed to living a full life, treating every day as a new day. It was these commitments that held us together. It was this bond that kept us uplifted in the face of a deteriorating planet outside our ranch gate.

I brought the same tracking techniques I used to track wolves in the wilderness into being a novice cattle rancher. I deepened my understanding of the role grazing animals played in the vibrancy of natural systems where waste ended up as food. The nutrient cycling from plants and minerals through the digestive tract of an animal fed the perennial grass plants that thrived in the cattle pastures Erik and I tended. Through ranching, we found ways to enhance and speed up the cycling of nutrients by allowing the cattle to create conditions for these perennial grass plants to thrive by mimicking the herd effect, similar to how the wolves moved the herds of elk in the wilderness areas where I tracked.

This form of ranching took on a new meaning for me. I had put myself in the footprints of the wolf when I tracked the animal, wanting to see and experience what the wolf did. Now I was intentionally playing the role of the wolf and our herd of cattle the role of the elk. I would even trot out like a wolf to the cattle pasture to move the herd from one area to the next, except without chasing them. Instead I used low-stress livestock handling, so the cattle would still have the effect on the land the elk did when moved from meadow to meadow by the wolves, but their meat would not get adrenaline surging through it and end up tasting like wild game. While I observed the pastures, I was able to draw upon the feelings and memories of the wilderness and make decisions that would lead me toward the outcome of land health, such as when to move the cattle and how long to allow pastures to recover before bringing the herd back in.

Our ranches contained the biodiversity similar to that of the places where the wild predator-prey relationships were thriving. The cattle managed holistically led to an increase in perennial grass plants. I then discovered that there was an entire world below my feet that was supporting the life above. Root systems of the perennial plants held the invisible network below the soil together with their roots. They were participating in a huge party with billions of life forms, all exchanging food and information beneath our feet faster than a Hollywood cocktail hour.

Nature holds the secrets of regeneration, as it holds the secrets to everything if you know how to look. I found there is no tool a human can make to replicate the functionality of the root system. When a cattle pasture has deep-rooting plants, the plants stay greener longer, build more soil, and hold more water within the soils. Those deep-rooted plants are always the first sought out by our cattle when they move into a fresh, recovered pasture. The perennial grass plants are like bowls of candy dotting the landscape and the cattle are like little kids with nothing holding them back from eating them. As soon as the animal bites that plant, the roots begin to shed off into the soil because there is no longer enough of the green plant to collect photosynthesis. The plant then puts energy into growing its roots and leaves back, to form new roots in the place of the ones that added carbon in the form of organic root matter into the soil and a new plant that will again feed the herds. With the energy from the sun, that cycle continues, a truly renewable energy source.

Root systems are so complex and far-reaching. Some trees have been found with roots growing two hundred feet deep, while a single rye plant can extend for a total of 372 miles and have over 6,000 miles of root hairs (Kourik 2008). All of these fibrous root hairs making their way into the soil protected by the layers of mycelium and humus hold the key to nutrient exchange between plants and the surrounding soil. The mycelium network of fungal threads is the interface for the roots and the nutrients. This network is the core fiber holding together the planet's soils. The mycelium forms a sort of neurological network of nature. It is found across the planet, under logs and bales of hay alike. Enveloping roots to extend the plant's ability to absorb nutrients and water from even farther distances than the roots themselves can reach, mycelium creates a fungal defense against invasive diseases to the plant while bringing food and nutrients that support our entire existence on this planet (Stamets 2005).

I found the pastures with the most fungal activity were also the most productive for grasses. I became an avid mushroom hunter, mainly to identify which conditions the pastures with a high percentage of mushrooms had that other pastures did not. The mushrooms were aiding greater diversity by contributing to the life cycles of birds, animals, and microorganisms.

While I was attending Prescott College, I traveled to the Hawaiian Islands to experience how Indigenous Hawaiians steward the land by tending their food source to persist many generations into the future. My goal was to come back and apply the philosophy I learned in Hawaii to the watershed where Erik and I lived. The Indigenous Hawaiian *ahupua'a*, which means a heap (*ahu*) surmounted by an image of a pig (*pua'a*), delineates the land encompassing their foodshed. Terracing foods from the mountains to the sea, these life-support systems are segments of land in the Hawaiian Islands that hold all the potential to support the people within. Divided into distinct zones, including the upland forest zone, the agriculture zone, and the coastal zone, these areas represent the biodiversity of a land being maximized by being vertically arranged. Within this *ahupua'a* design, both productive wildlands and agricultural lands hold a place for food production and consumption. What historic Indigenous Hawaiians did not forage from their own *ahupua'a*, they traded with others. It was what Erik and I strived to create in our land and life in California.

While visiting the island of Kauai, I met Ipo and Kamahalo, who were in the process of starting a nature-based school called Kanuikapono. The vision of the school is to cultivate the twenty-first century *ahupua'a*, grounded in Indigenous education and community renewal. Ipo, an attractive woman of Hawaiian and Filipino descent, shared with me that when Hawaiians were living in intact ahupua'a land divisions, there was always an abundance of food. There was so much that any passing ship that came by the islands would leave full of food from the island. This kept the peace, as there was never scarcity.

Erik and I also dreamed of producing abundant food that we could share with our community. Our dreams were big, and we built a solid foundation from which to launch them. We moved from Broken Arrow Ranch, to the neighboring Toto Ranch, just a mile as the hawk flies from the ocean, to build our homestead. We left behind fruit trees and perennial plants as a gift for the future generations, as I had at every place I'd lived.

Our dreams grew and were formulated to hold together our lives according to what we valued most. This formed our holistic context, which directs our daily decisions as well as our big dreams. It is a guidepost for both our family and our business as ranchers. The holistic context balances out our quality of life, the system and behaviors needed to produce that quality of life, as well as our future resource base of how we are leaving this earth better than we found it. Our context reads:

Our mission is to steward grasslands by mimicking natural systems through regenerative agriculture practices. We hold the vision to keep the home fire burning with strong family values of love for each other and the earth. We will make a big impact for the future generations by influencing large-scale restoration of watersheds and the grasslands within them while producing nutrient-dense food for thousands of families.

We will accomplish our mission and vision through ranching. Erik has a deep-rooted lineage of ranching and Doniga also fell in love with the lifestyle of being with family, the land, and making a difference with agriculture practices that feed the people and the planet.

We value keeping our bodies, minds, and spirits healthy so we can take care of others. We will take the time to eat meals together prepared from the land. We will read, play, and enjoy each other's company. We will give each other the space to immerse in creative projects and time in the wilderness. We will travel to see beautiful places and immerse in different cultures.

We will be a part of nature and the regeneration of biodiversity. We will build healthy soil more and more every year.

We will teach our children values of love for one another, appreciation for the earth, and the drive to follow their passion.

I realized for the first time that although my birthplace in the Snoqualmie Valley was where my heart first found home, my true home turned out to be with Erik, building a family and participating in the most commonplace actions of growing food and nurturing one another. I found my soulmate by tracking a mountain lion in the watershed where Erik was born and raised. Together we found our path through inner-tracking, looking in each corner of our past and prejudices and not dwelling on those. We created new possibilities each day for our life together.

Family

After my marriage to Erik and the bonding of our two lives together, the natural progression was to bring new life to the world. My first pregnancy, like 25 percent of pregnancies, ended with a miscarriage, which was devastatingly sad. In time, however, we welcomed Larry Lyle Londolozi, Quill Dawn Chorus, and Quince Dyani Chante Markegard to our family, which already included Lea. They were all birthed at home, and each labor and delivery brought me closer to nature.

After Quince was born, something unexpected happened to me. I suffered from postpartum depression. I didn't think anything could rescue me from the despair and pain I felt. Gilbert Walking Bull taught me that with strong vision and intentions, we can accomplish anything, but my agony was profound and without a real cause I could point to. I should have been elated after bringing so much new life into the world. Instead, I entered into a darkness in which I could not fathom the light outside my window. I was having difficulty drawing on the lessons on how to improve my mental state that I had learned from Gilbert. I stopped brushing my hair, wearing clean clothes, and taking care of myself. Instead of feeling more connected with all the life on earth, as I'd expected, I felt completely cut off from it.

Erik knew he had to do something. He had a plane ticket to his family reunion, but instead of leaving me, he missed his flight to come home with a surprise. He bought me my first jersey cow, Daisy, and the rhythm she brought to my life—waking early to milk her at dawn—brought me back to myself.

Daisy quickly became part of the family. With her dark eyes and long eyelashes, which drew everyone in, she became the symbolic healer of our family. Waking up early every morning, I now had a task that was all my own, like a morning meditation, similar to my travels to my old secret spot by the pond. I couldn't be late getting my boots on and walking out to have my morning alone with Daisy. The steady rhythmic motion of hand milking, alternating my left and right palms as I pressed my cheek against Daisy's flank, set my brain back into balance and over a matter of weeks lifted my depression.

I decided that my children would be a part of the healing rhythms of ranching too and I would put them right work with me to raise as many animals as we could.

Erik and I had already begun direct marketing our grass-fed beef and lamb, which we raised on the coastal pastures of our ranch. Families flocked to us when we sent out an announcement that we were selling the only local source of grass-fed meats. Markegard Family Grass-Fed soon became a household name amongst our larger community, who loved the taste and nutrition of our meats.

When it came time for lambing, all the kids, especially Lea, were on close watch as the fragile newborns were birthed. Every season there are typically one or two lambs born too weak or their mothers abandon them. Lea knew what to look for when she walked out one foggy morning when she was only eight years old. Droopy ears, head down, difficulty getting up to nurse, and eyes that lack a brightness are the signs she looked for. Lea walked out into the pasture with a keen eye for saving a life. She found a lamb that was the runt and just did not have enough energy to get the first colostrum from the ewe. Lea picked up that lamb, warmed it next to her body, and bottle-fed the colostrum we had saved from a different ewe as she sat in the kitchen. Soon another member of the family joined us at meal times, clicking on the hardwood floors with small hooves. The lamb would sound a soft bleating when she was ready for her next bottle. Following Lea around everywhere she went, the lamb had a new mom and slept in a cardboard box at the foot of her bed. Lea awoke every four hours to bring the lamb a warm bottle. She held her lamb in close and the bond of child and animal formed. Lea at fourteen continues to rescue runts.

We went on to start an organic egg and pastured pork

enterprise my son Larry coined Green Eggs and Ham. Two hundred laying hens lived out on our pastures and we converted a stock trailer to hold nesting boxes, roosts, and chicken doors with ramps. The trailer was pulled out to a new patch of pasture each day. The chicken trailer followed the cattle on their moves from pasture to pasture. Pecking through the cow pies they discovered grass seeds and fly larvae. They spread the cow pies throughout the pasture, like a well-scattered compost application. The pecked-through cow manure along with the chicken poop was a perfect balance of the addition of nitrogen, phosphorus, potassium and other nutrients to a field. As we brought the chickens to the pasture it was as if we were filling the role the band-tailed pigeons once played when they flew in such great numbers, each depositing fertilizer upon the lands. When mammals and birds were abundant so was their manure. This in turn kick-started the carbon cycle and the ability for the lands to retain water. By bringing back birds and grazers, we were also bringing fertility to the grasslands.

Later we added chickens and goats for meat and expanded our cattle and sheep herds. Our main driver was to ensure that all of the animals were able to express their inherent traits of being a pig, chicken, cow, goat, or sheep. They ate a diet they were designed to eat and they inhabited lands they were built to inhabit. Understanding the complexity of nature's template for raising animals took all of my training in wilderness awareness and Erik's experience as a rancher. We listened to the language of nature. The plans we made took in all the factors of seasonality. Our design of how we raised our animals was cyclical, with each component connected to the next. The result of this type of agriculture was that the carbon was in situ, never leaving the ground, but instead building from place and allowing the natural cycles of birth, growth, death, and decay to regenerate the pastures. The health of the soil flourished as a result and was directly linked to the health of our family.

My daughter Quill, back from feeding her chickens, is reciting the seven sacred principles. She relates the most with *Wo-wa unsi-la*, or maybe she just likes saying it, the way it rolls off her tongue like a song. The phrase means "caring for all living creatures," and is meant to ensure that each interaction with all the species is beneficial to that species. I explained to Quill that it is like when she is gathering branches to make a fairy crown, and she must first observe and ask the tree if she can harvest its branches, then listen to the tree to see if she gets a response. If the branch is important for the tree to bear fruit then she needs to leave the branch. If the branch should be removed to let in more light to the center of the tree then she should do her part in caring for that tree and remove the branch. Quill recited the word like a chant, "*Wo-wa unsi-la*, caring for all living things," skipping and singing with her face raised up to the sky like a wolf pup. Earlier, over the dinner table, we each recited these attributes and reflected on how we can improve and how we did throughout the day on truly encompassing the teachings. When Larry built a bow out of a limb on a bay tree earlier in the day, he showed *Wo-bli-he-cha*: he was engaged in every moment with pure satisfaction in his process. The last sacred attribute, *Wi-co-za-ni*, is the sacred state of health, which often begins in the mind and positive thinking, one which we all strive for; however, it takes all of the other attributes to fall in place to achieve *Wi-co-za-ni*. The life we've created here on the ranch, holistic context in place, has created the conditions for all of those attributes to blossom inside each of us.

Earlier in the day, the first thing I did was to jog out to the front of the ranch where the dairy cows were in their grazing pasture to bring them in for milking. Nearly a mile on uneven terrain, skirting around brush and jumping over ravines, I paid attention to the life around me. Seeds clung to the tarweed plants, which were still green despite many dry months. I reached down to touch the soft seed of a thistle plant, smooth to the touch with a sheen that resembled silk. On a foggy summer morning the grasses are dry; however, we moved the cattle into a pasture with a high percentage of California oatgrass and purple needle grass, both native bunchgrasses that pull water up that is stored in the soil. The green plants provide the cows with much-needed protein later into the dry season. It is a longer walk to come in every day for milking, and the cows don't always get the cue that their milking parlor awaits them.

Our dairy herd is larger now. Milk cows have come and gone, but Daisy, that first cow that Erik came home with, is still with the herd. I found her and Annabelle, the other Jersey, grazing with the two lively Guernsey heifers. With coats of light brown, like the color of oak furniture, with white blotches, the Guernsey cows, Bluebell and Buttercup, each have a distinct pattern displaying their own identity. Daisy, ten years old, was starting to show her age. At the back of the group she walked slowly, carefully conserving her energy, traveling along the contour of the hill, not meandering from her path.

Walking back with the four ladies, the herder instinct was awoken in my brain. As I walked behind the small group of hoofed megafauna, bringing them in to be milked—an act that humans began over ten thousand years ago with the domestication of livestock—my body felt the connection to the earth and emotions of happiness overcame me.

In the faint light of dawn, a coyote sounded a barking howl in the distance. I quickened my step. There were newborn calves in the pasture where the coyote was sounding the loud bark. I heard our two dogs, Luta and Nuka, barking from the safety of the barnyard in response to the coyote. The two Australian shepherds, who stand slightly smaller than a coyote, have come to know they are no match for their wild cousin. Entering the barnyard, Suzanna asked if she should go up on the four-wheeler and chase away the coyote. She saw the calves running. My step quickened to a run. I told her I would go and I began to run up the steep incline above our house toward the sound of the coyote. I climbed over the split redwood fence that delineates our little patch of human inhabitancy and I entered into the wild grasslands. The coyote continued to sound a barking howl, loud and echoing through the rolling grassy hills.

The hill in front of me blocked my view of the animal, but as I reached the apex I saw her standing there. She was facing east, barking and howling loudly, not disturbed at first by my presence. The calves were not running in fear; they were frolicking amongst the moms, playfully. The dogs did not follow me, most likely because they did not want to start a squabble over territory. Now less than twenty yards away, I approached to see how close the coyote would let me get. Obviously her attention was turned in a different direction. Possibly she was protecting her den, which sat in the southern-facing eucalyptus canyon above our house. We had tracked the den site and at times found pups' chew toys adorning the entrance of the holes, slightly taller than they were wide, dug into the slope. It reminded me of the rendezvous site I found that day in the Idaho wilderness tracking wolves. Even things that had been stolen from the barnyard, like work gloves, lay strewn and chewed close to the entrance. Maybe it was a way for the coyotes to show they were outsmarting our dogs—by stealing things from under their noses. It was the wrong time of year for pups, but the right time of year for breeding. If this was the alpha, she may have been reinforcing her hierarchy in order to dissuade other coyotes from breeding. The period of courtship amongst coyotes, called *proestrus*, is the longest of any canine, signifying that the bond between the alpha pair is especially important (Elbroch and Rinehart 2011).

The coyote turned and slowly trotted, stopping in the middle of the pasture. The mother cows paid little attention to the coyote as they chewed the dry grasses. Nuka apprehensively appeared by my side as Suzanna walked up the hill to join me. Just as they arrived, the coyote scratched the ground with all four feet. Left rear foot timed with right front foot and right rear foot timed with left front, she scratched the grass, kicking up some dirt. She continued to bark and howl, and then journeyed to the other side of the pasture, briefly glancing back at us. Was she communicating territory or possibly calling out to a mate to elicit breeding? The location she chose to scratch and leave scent from the scent glands between her toes was a prominent place on a small hill next to the intersection of the ranch road and the straight trail she traveled toward the eucalyptus trees.

I often track the coyotes in the silt of the ranch road; the substrate portrays every detail of the wild canines' tracks, the wrinkles in the pad and the sharp pricks of the claws. Scat also lines the ranch road and accumulates at the top of the hill in a large latrine. One day Larry and I counted twenty scats from coyotes of all different ages. Living in a place where there are no longer wolves, I often turn to the coyote, as their closest relative. I have tracked coyote in the middle of cities and on edges of suburban neighborhoods. It reminds me that I do not need to be deep in the wilderness to find that connection to the wild. The coyotes travel the edges, they take part in the cycle of life and death. They can be a symbol of that wild that still remains no matter how much humans have paved over their homes and bulldozed the fragments of habitat amongst the high-rises.

As I head back to the milking parlor I contemplate our role as regenerative ranchers. Things are out of balance. Many of the interactions that once kept the grasslands healthy, the large predators that moved the herds of prey that in turn impacted the health of the plants, the songbirds, and all life on the prairie, are now gone. As I learned from the wolf, it is my time now to tend to my family as nature tends to hers. I have the responsibility to feed my children and nurture the wild they have inside. I work to retain and protect wild spaces and wild patterns within us and around us, making space for the wildness we and all our kin need to survive and thrive.

Three things you can track almost anywhere

No matter where in the world you are, you can find these three things to track—and doing so will get you in tune with the rhythms and behaviors of the wildlife near you. Remember that tracking is about noticing signs and asking questions; it can take a long time before answers start coming to you. Keep your senses and your mind open!

PREDATOR

Research which predators live in your area. Some of those predators for me are coyotes, mountain lions, grey foxes, and birds of prey; in your neighborhood you may find skunks, raccoons, bobcats, wolves, bears, or river otters. Even in New York City, there are hawks in the skies and coyotes in Central Park.

Then narrow down your hunt: Do you know whether your predator prefers to be near water, and is there a river, lake, or maybe a hidden spring in your area?

Look for trails. Often it is difficult to see the tracks, because of the soft pads of the toes and heel, unless the trails go by a mud puddle or the bank of a stream. When you look around you will begin to see trails that are worn in that may cross or travel along the human trails. You might find scat along those trails, as a territorial scent marking. Follow those trails to see where they lead you and what clues you pick up along the way.

Often the predator is the keystone species of an area. They are the ones that help keep the whole ecological system together, and without that keystone predator, things would look different. Plants might get overgrazed and certain life would disappear altogether. So when you track a predator, you are also tracking the whole interconnected web of life, such as the smallest insect that may depend on remains of the carcasses that the predator leaves behind.

PREY

What does your area's predator eat? Are there certain things that are abundant, like voles, squirrels, or mice that both the ground and aerial predators are feasting on? Are there larger prey animals such as deer in your area?

Deer live in a variety of habitat, from the mountains to the cities. They can be one of the most rewarding animals to track. Their cloven hooves make sharp lines in the shape of a heart, and at times you can see the dewclaws, two smaller indents, just behind the hoof. If you find a deer track, trace your fingers along the edge of the track, getting to know the size and shape. Feel the edges and then feel how deep the tracks sink in. Then look ahead on the trail and try to find another track about eighteen to twenty-six inches in front of the one you are feeling. See how many tracks you can find and where the trail will lead you. Start to notice other signs such as deer droppings, antler rubs on branches, or evidence of feeding on nearby plants.

PLANTS

Look up close to any patch of plants and you'll likely find that some of them have been bitten. Does it look like they were torn or clipped? Deer only have bottom incisors, so they leave the plants rough and torn. Rabbits, on the other hand, have sharp top and bottom incisors, leaving the plants they eat clean and at a 45 degree angle, almost like it has been cut with a knife. Once you get to know the plants and trees in your area, find out when they produce fruit or nuts. When do the plum trees fruit? When do the acorns from the oak trees ripen? There will be certain times of year that all the herbivores are feasting on the abundant crop of fruit or nuts in a feeding frenzy. That is a good time to track the plants and find out what it looks like when a squirrel eats an acorn versus when a bird like a woodpecker or jay eats an acorn.

Once you have tracked a predator, a prey, and a plant then move on to finding more tracks. You can also put together a master list of local animals by using field guides and range maps. Start with listing all the mammals that are in your range. You can then move on to birds, plants, fungi, insects, reptiles, and amphibians. Getting to know your neighbors can help you to feel more at home yourself.

Fire

A fire burned as people began to gather. A large pot of soup I prepared the night before sat on the burning flame, full of onions, chicken broth, squash, and Daisy's sweet cream. The one thing that separates us as humans from the rest of our mammal kin: we cook.

We stood in a circle, fifty people who had gathered for a meal on the ranch. We gave thanks for all of creation that selflessly gave sustenance. We gave thanks for gathering all together and the dance of the flames as we listened to the crackling of the redwood branches ablaze, a hungry fire devouring the wood like a wolf eating its kill. We sent thanksgiving and greeting out to all life on earth as well as the unseen powers that move through all things. The hunger we felt couldn't be met by just a meal. We were hungry for the gathering, for sharing stories, for feeling the land around us embodied in the food we ate.

The long table outside our front step was full of laughter,

people sharing stories, and kids running to grab a slice of bread to take to the fire and warm on a stick. We ate greens, both wild and farmed, raw and cooked. Smoke rose up from the coals and the smell of venison grilling wafted across the long table that stretched around the front and side of our yellow farmhouse. The strips of venison were sliced thinly to reveal a crimson center gradually fading into a burnt umber. We all experienced something primordial when we tasted the venison. Knowing the land where the buck grazed and where Erik took the life of the deer with gratitude and reverence brought the story of the land inside our bodies. The fire brought out the enticing taste, and we considered that humans have been in relationship in this way with deer and fire since the beginning.

After we ate, I stood at the end of the arching table and called everyone's attention. I told the crowd, "From the coast of California to the pebbled shores of Lake Ontario, tribes are gathered to protect our most basic need for clean water." I glanced at the decanters on the table filled with water from the spring on the ranch. "Imagine if the water we're drinking tonight was tainted with highly volatile oil that was being fracked on land that was once lush prairie that supported the venison and greens on your plate. Similar struggles over clean water and unpolluted lands are happening all over the world. Common people like us are struggling to live a life where they can drink the water, know what is being put in their food, and raise their children where there is a future of living on this planet in the most commonplace harmonious way. We were invited by our Native American friends to assist in the protection of the water here on the continent called Turtle Island. So Erik will be traveling to Standing Rock to bring winter supplies to the water protectors."

Over warm apple persimmon crisp topped with fresh whipped cream, we finished the evening feeling our hunger had indeed been met: not just by the food, but by the stories we had told, the community we belonged to, and our shared commitment to caring for all of our kin.

I stayed at the ranch to care for the animals and the children when Erik traveled to Standing Rock. He phoned me the first night to give me an update. As Erik approached the Oceti Sakowin, meaning Seven Council Fires camp, at Standing Rock, which was laid out in the shape of a buffalo skull with the Missouri River as the backdrop, he became part of a history that will be told for many generations to come. It had been nearly 150 years since the Native American tribes of the region had gathered, and they marked this historical event by setting up their tepees in this symbolic manner, to honor the buffalo. The dance that once took place between the Indigenous people and the buffalo regenerated the perennial life on the prairie, and of course it's the model we're striving to mimic on our own lands. The role of predators, including humans, moving the herbivores through the grasslands to regenerate soils and biodiversity.

Erik told me that when he approached the fire in the center of camp to bring the wall tents, butchery knives, tables, and chairs to Winona Kasto's Traditional Foods Kitchen, which fed hundreds of people each day, two deer carcasses had arrived at the same time as him. The kitchen crew was grateful for the extra supplies as they quickly used the butcher knife to break down the deer and to hang strips of the meat on a rack for jerky. A large fifty-gallon pot sat on a fire, corn hung from rafters, and herbs were laid out in a dehydrator all to feed the water protectors.

Erik went to assist the Spirit Riders and their horses, the young men who rode their horses to the front lines of the protest to attempt to halt the construction of the pipeline. As a rancher, Erik immediately found kinship with the horses and their riders. Placed at the tip of the buffalo horn, the Hunk-pati, or Crow Creek tribe, formed the camp of Spirit Riders. Thirteen young men, all with horses, were part of a larger group of Spirit Riders who rode every year in memory of 38+2 of their chiefs and holy men who were hanged in the largest one-day mass execution in US history, on December 26, 1862. They say 38+2 because at first it was only 38, and then shortly after two more were found and killed. Erik assisted the Spirit Riders in building a winter shelter for the horses. Erik and Greg Grey Cloud, the horse manager for the Spirit Riders, got to work designing a windbreak and purchasing supplies, and within the first few hours of them beginning the work on the shelter, the horses began to gather. That night was met with freezing temperatures combined with a wind chill that would make any animal seek out shelter.

As ranchers, we stood with the people of Standing Rock to protect the sacred. There is still so much for us to learn from Indigenous tribes as we go about our work of stewarding lands and feeding people. If we are to produce food and withstand climate change, the most pressing threat to our world, then we need to use every drop of wisdom we can learn from those who have lived close to the earth, treating each species as kin. Standing Rock reminded us that traditional wisdom combined with appropriate renewable energy technology is the only way to move forward in a world where people in power are driven by profit alone. Only the movement of millions can create a future where our children, many generations to come, can have the privilege of drinking from streams and rivers of pure water, walking amongst an intact prairie or old-growth forest and knowing that it was their relatives who made it all possible.

The fire that burned in the center of camp, keeping the water protectors warm and fed, was the same fire inside those who gathered to stand up for their right for pure water.

When Erik returned from Standing Rock, our first frost of the season also arrived. It was as if Erik had brought some of the cold of North Dakota to the shores of the Pacific. The cold also marked an end to a search that had been underway in the Parvati Valley of India, high in the Himalayas, for one of my dear classmates from the Wilderness Awareness School,

Justin Alexander, who had danced the mountain lion around our fires and captured the flag in the scout game.

The last time I saw Justin was in a chance encounter in a San Francisco hotel lobby in 2012. He had just flown in from LA and was checking in at the hotel as I was leaving with Erik's mother, who was staying there. We looked at each other after not seeing one another for nearly ten years and immediately were reminded of our bond in our youth and our common language of nature. Since then, I occasionally read his blog, *Adventures of Justin*, witnessing as his own search for freedom took him to live with the Mentawai in Indonesia, the Dhokpas (the last remaining Tibetan nomads), and in the end to Himalayan caves with a Naga Baba, or Hindu holy man. I was not surprised to see that our time at WAS, immersing in nature, had fed in each of us a yearning for freedom and authenticity.

Justin never lost the spirit of adventure, of pushing himself to his physical, mental, and spiritual limits. I can't help but think he was fulfilling what we all had dreamt of when we were teenagers in the wilderness of Washington, to be like the legendary Apache scouts and be able to go anywhere in the world and survive in the wild. Eighteen years following our training, he walked out into one of the most unforgiving landscapes and never returned. Sometimes when people are given the tools to fly, they never put their feet back on the ground.

We lit a sacred fire for Justin at dawn. I could almost picture all of us as youth sitting around that fire, telling jokes, talking about the mysteries of our tracking adventures, and singing songs. Anne, our WAS mentor, came. The group of us from WAS had not kept in touch often, as each of us forged our own path, yet when we did come across each other, it felt as if no time had passed since our days in the woods, by those earlier fires. We told stories of the great adventures we had together and with Justin. Some classmates sent messages. Terry Skyped in from Seattle and told of a time when he'd spent the day with Justin on the beach on his seventeenth birthday. Justin had made sure Terry had the time of his life. Terry, now the director of a circus and an acrobat for Teatro ZinZanni, says he developed his passion for circus by learning animal forms around the fire at WAS with all of us, and watching Cirque du Soleil on our long road trips in Chris's Suburban. Greg messaged from Berlin. Still tracking daily and teaching kids at a forest school, he gave me a report on the wolves in Germany. They have come back strong, possibly even leaving their scats on those statues as the biologist had hoped. They are repopulating a country that at one point was the center of the hatred towards wolves and now has strict laws to protect the species.

The sacred fire we lit for Justin is a tradition of the Odawa people and was brought to us at WAS by Paul Raphael, a peacemaker for the tribe on the Upper Peninsula in Michigan. A young man, Liam, who was trained as a fire tender, came to our ranch and lit a fire as a connection to the ancestors, so that people who knew Justin could gather by the flames and release the agony, grieve for their loss. The fire became our connection to spirit, our light in the darkness, and a pathway to the unknown.

As the sacred fire died down, we released our friend Justin, who had spent all those years with us in the wilderness, and who had now entered the decay stage of the life cycle, as we all will in time. We knew that just as his body would return nutrients to the earth, the memories of our time together, the rites of passages we went through as teens, and those timeless moments around the fire in the wet Western Washington wilderness will continue as memories, and our stories will live on, nourishing us and our descendants. We learned to live like wild animals so that we could make a difference in the future. Our time together shaped us, and we are all in our own way striving to find the meaning of life and death, the best way for humans to interact with this beautiful planet. With Justin's disappearance, with the loss of a man who cared deeply for this earth, more responsibility lands on the rest of us.

There may be a time that things get worse, when rain will not fall on endless deserts and birds will no longer come to deposit seeds and feces because there is no food for them. But for now, we have so much to be grateful for. For now, the beavers remember how to be beavers. They build the pools and wetlands that will in turn bring dragonflies, frogs, birds, and newts. The birds remember how to be birds. They deposit tiny seeds that will grow into giant redwood trees. The salmon remember how to be salmon, running up streams until the streams are colored red by the fish and shaded by the redwood forests. Herbivores remember how to be herbivores, moving across vast prairies, disturbing and fertilizing the ground. The grasses remember how to be grasses. They capture the carbon and hold it where it belongs, in the soil. The soils of the prairie and forests remember how to be soils. They continue to host billions of organisms in a small spoonful. Those billions of organisms are also held in the bodies of humans, making it possible for us all to live.

It appears that it's up to humans to remember, right now, what it means to be humans. We need to remember how to live in reciprocity with our kin, to respect and honor this beautiful world and all its inhabitants, before everything we depend on and everything that depends on us is lost. As long as we remember, dawn again will come and the sun will continue to provide the energy for life.

Anne brought pictures of our time in Alaska, the trip where I'd been with wolves for the first time, where I'd found my pack after being led there by a white wolf. There were also pictures of my classmates and me beating drums and dancing the deer, dressed in buckskins we had tanned and sewn into clothes using the sinew from the deer as thread. We were all smiling and laughing in the pictures, wild inside and out. Anne also brought a basket I had made her, woven of willow branches.

Holding that basket woven next to the Snoqualmie River so long ago, I held a symbol of my life. I remembered so vividly the unskilled hands I'd brought to weaving at first, the way the patterns of weaving, the sensitivity with which I had to choose the right materials, had calmed me and helped me focus my intentions. I wove my life together on the banks of that river, sitting for hours alone in the silence.

With the basket cradled in my hands, I realized that all of my intentions for my life—communing with my wild kin, having a family, impacting the planet positively, and being part of a larger network of regeneration—had come to fruition. Every single piece of my life, disparate as they all may have seemed, had come together to form a cohesive, useful, sturdy whole.

Those wild branches that grew near my birthplace had woven my life basket, still bound together after all those years.

Epilogue

It is 2019 and an enormous youth climate strike is underway. My daughter Quill, now eleven years old, is just like me: strong willed, on the rebellious side, and full of passion and purpose. When I explain to her what is going on and we watch a few videos of the youth leading this movement, she immediately perks up. We make plans to bring her and her friend Zoe to San Francisco the next day to take to the streets. Quill paints signs reading *We demand climate justice* and *Youth for our future*. Taking the train into the city, we are immediately joined with hundreds and then thousands of diverse youth arriving for the same purpose. They have walked out of school to demand those in power take action to protect the quality of life for the future generations. The energy is vibrant. One teenage girl shouts on a loudspeaker, directing the group as they gather in front of Nancy Pelosi's office, the first woman to be speaker of the house. The crowd is diverse, kids of all ages from different backgrounds all unifying around a message to care for the earth. At first Quill and Zoe are timid; for country kids this is a lot of stimulation. Once the marching starts we all feel the power. We all begin chanting. *Hey-ho, climate change has got to go.* Quill holds her sign up high as we approach the next stop, Bank of America. The message is for these large corporations to divest from fossil fuels. The youth across the globe are mobilizing. Like Standing Rock, first initiated by Indigenous youth, this movement is led by the next generation, who see what their future holds if climate change is not addressed immediately. It is time for all ages to listen and support.

I know the time will come when Quill will spread her wings in search of her own place amongst this tornado of life. She lit up about joining the groups that organize the Fridays for the Future and the following week she walked out of school again, to the nearby elementary school where the older kids had organized a speech for the younger kids to educate on climate change. It is the yearning for something more and a rebellion against the lack of adult actions to address climate change that have lit the fire inside our youth. My hope is that this movement will lead youth toward purpose and meaning, much like what I was searching for when I ran away from home. There is now a vibrant youth movement where they can direct their inner tornado and project that feeling through their voices and actions. They will be heard. They are remembering what their brains and intuition have never forgotten, just like the beaver and the songbird.

It is now my time to step aside and allow the next wolf girl to shine. I have led my children to nature, where they know they can always go for solace and learn the most important lessons in life, just like I did from the wolf.

Quill knows that when she gets on her horse and we move the cattle to a new pasture she is the wolf girl. She is moving her cattle just like the wolves moved the elk. This holds a solution for climate change. The carbon sequestration results are staggering when the herds are intentionally moved by stewards of the land. Our ranch land sequesters thousands of tonnes of carbon per year, as opposed to our neighbor's ranch land, which releases carbon because it is not managed to mimic nature. And not only is the land healthier and more diverse, but the humans interacting with nature and their food are healthier. When Quill is out on her horse galloping through the grassland she is experiencing both the thrill of being fully alive and the knowing that she is being of service to the greater whole. Other times, when Quill is having a difficult time and feeling turmoil inside, she must take a walk by herself amongst the grasses and the trees. She comes back with a different look in her eye; a healing takes place amongst the grasses. She knows she can always turn to nature, to her secret spot, to talk with the trees and be curious about life.

The rites of passage in our culture from youth to adult can involve walking amongst the wild and connecting with the animals, being curious about all life on this earth. That curiosity will lead to passion and ultimately to a purpose or vision. When Quill has discovered her vision, she will wake up in the morning with a drive and a fire inside. I can see her wild within. The inner wildness of youth is not something to be tamed, especially not now. It is time to tend to that wild, like a tinder bundle ready to burst into flames. Because it is that wild, that passion of the 7.6 million people across the globe in 150 different countries who participated in the September 2019 climate marches, that will lead us back. It will lead us back to tending to all our relatives, to finding the solutions to the climate crisis we face. And when the wild within us brings back the wild within nature, we will be living our true human purpose.

References

Anderson, M. Kat. 2005. *Tending the Wild: Native American Knowledge and the Management of California's Natural Resources.* Berkeley, Los Angeles, London: University of California Press.

Bellows, Barbara. 2001. "Nutrient Cycling in Pastures." Publication for Appropriate Technology Transfer for Rural Areas. <http://pss.uvm.edu/pdpforage/Materials/SoilFert/nutrient-cycling.pdf>

Callenbach, Ernest. 1996. *Bring Back the Buffalo!: A Sustainable Future for America's Great Plains.* Berkeley, Los Angeles, London: University of California Press.

Crystal, Ellie. 1997. "Mac Wirema Korako Ruka, Spiritual Elder of the Waitaha Maori of New Zealand, and Jim Yellow Horse Man, Cherokee Elder, Interview with Ellie Crystal." <crystalinks.com/macki.html>

Descartes, René. 1644. *Principles of Philosophy.*

Doidge, Norman. 2016. *The Brain's Way of Healing.* New York: Penguin Books.

Elbroch, Mark, and Kurt Rinehart. 2011. *Behavior of North American Mammals.* New York: Houghton Mifflin Harcourt.

ETC Group. 2014. "With Climate Chaos, Who Will Feed Us?" Action Group on Erosion, Technology, and Concentration. <etcgroup.org/content/who-will-feed-us-0>

Food and Agriculture Organization of the United Nations (FAO). 2014. "Agriculture's Greenhouse Gas Emissions on the Rise." Food and Agriculture Organization of the United Nations, April 11. <fao.org/news/story/en/item/216137/icode>

Gunders, Dana. 2012. "Wasted: How America Is Losing Up to 40 Percent of Its Food from Farm to Fork to Landfill." (NRDC Issue Paper.) <https://www.nrdc.org/sites/default/files/wasted-food-IP.pdf>

"Historical Timeline — Farmers & the Land," *Growing a Nation: The Story of American Agriculture,* accessed May 23, 2017 <agclassroom.org/gan/timeline/farmers_land.htm>

Hofferth, S. L, and J. F. Sandberg. 2001. "How American Children Spend Their Time." *Journal of Marriage and Family* 63 (3): 295–308. <doi.org/10.1111/j.1741-3737.2001.00295.x>

Inglish, Patty. 2017. "South Pacific—the Maori People of New Zealand." *Owlcation*, March 12. <owlcation.com/social-sciences/Aborigines-New-Zealand>

International Forum for Agroecology. 2015. "Report for the International Forum for Agroecology." Sélingué, Mali. <foodsovereignty.org/wp-content/uploads/2015/10/NYE-LENI-2015-ENGLISH-FINAL-WEB.pdf>

IUCN, Conservation International, and NatureServe. 2004. "Global Amphibian Assessment." <natureserve.org/library/amphibian_fact_sheet.pdf>

Juneau, Denise. 2010. "Flathead Reservation Timeline Confederated Salish and Kootenai Tribes." (Montana Tribal Histories Timeline.) Montana Office of Public Instruction. <opi.mt.gov/pdf/IndianEd/IEFA/FlatheadTimeline.pdf>

Kourik, Robert. 2008. *Roots Demystified*. Occidental: Metamorphic Press.

Lange, Greg. 2003. "Smallpox Epidemic of 1862 among Northwest Coast and Puget Sound Indians." *History Link*. <historylink.org/File/5171>

Lewis, Deane. 2015. "Owl Eyes and Vision." *The Owl Pages*, June 25. <owlpages.com/owls/articles.php?a=5>

Liebenberg, Louis. 1990. *The Art of Tracking: The Origin of Science*. Southern Africa: David Philip Publishers (Pty) Ltd.

Mollison, Bill. 1998. *Permaculture: A Designers' Manual*. Tyalgum, Australia: Tagari Publications.

Moskowitz, David. 2013. *Wolves in the Land of Salmon*. Portland: Timber Press.

Muir, John. 1911. *My First Summer in the Sierra*. Boston: Houghton Mifflin Company.

National Park Service (NPS). 2010. *Historic Resource Study for Golden Gate National Recreation Area in San Mateo County*. U.S. Department of the Interior. Redwood City, CA: San Mateo County Historic Association.

National Snow and Ice Data Center. 2017. "Facts about Glaciers." Boulder, Colorado: National Snow and Ice Data Center. <nsidc.org/cryosphere/glaciers/quickfacts.html>

O'Mara, F. P. 2012. "The Role of Grasslands in Food Security and Climate Change." *Annals of Botany* 110 (6): 1263–1270. <dx.doi.org/10.1093/aob/mcs209>

Panunzi, Eleonora. 2008. "Are Grasslands Under Threat?" Data analysis for Food and Agriculture Organization. <fao.org/ag/agp/agpc/doc/grass_stats/grass-stats.htm>

Pimentel, David, and Michael Burgess. 2013. "Soil Erosion Threatens Food Production." *Agriculture* 3 (3): 443–463. <dx.doi.org/10.3390/agriculture3030443>

Ripple, W. J., and R. L. Beschta. 2012. "Trophic Cascades in Yellowstone: The First 15 Years After Wolf Reintroduction." *Biological Conservation* 145 (1): 205–213. <doi.org/10.1016/j.biocon.2011.11.005>

Russell, Stephen. 2014. "Everything You Need to Know About Agricultural Emissions." World Resources Institute. <wri.org/blog/2014/05/everything-you-need-know-about-agricultural-emissions>

Salmón, Enrique. 2000. "Kincentric Ecology: Indigenous Perceptions of the Human-Nature Relationship." *Ecological Applications* 10 (5): 1327–1332.

Savory, Allan. 1999. *Holistic Management: A New Framework for Decision Making.* Washington, DC: Island Press.

Shaffer, Joyce. 2012. "Neuroplasticity and Positive Psychology in Clinical Practice: A Review for Combined Benefits." *Psychology* 3 (12A): 1110-1115.

Shaw, Mary Lou. 2013. "Keeping Heritage Breeds: Dutch Belted Milking Cows." *Mother Earth News*, January.

Sobrevila, Claudia. 2008. *The Role of Indigenous Peoples in Biodiversity Conservation: The Natural but Often Forgotten Partners.* Washington, DC: The World Bank.

Stamets, Paul. 2005. *Mycelium Running: How Mushrooms Can Help Save the World.* Berkeley: Ten Speed Press.

Stewart, Hilary. 1984. *Cedar.* Seattle: University of Washington Press.

Swamp, Chief Jake. 1995. *Giving Thanks: A Native American Good Morning Message.* New York: Lee and Low Books Inc.

Teague, W. R., S. Apfelbaum, R. Lal, U. P. Kreuter, J. Rowntree, C. A. Davies, R. Conser, M. Rasmussen, J. Hatfield, T. Wang, F. Wang, and P. Byck. 2016. "The Role of Ruminants in Reducing Agriculture's Carbon Footprint in North America." *Journal of Soil and Water Conservation* 71 (2): 156–164.

Thompson, E., A. M. Harper, and S. Kraus. 2008. "San Francisco Foodshed Assessment: Think Globally Act Locally." Davis, CA: American Farmland Trust, 2008.

Ward, Mary H., Jay Lubin, James Giglierano, Joanne S. Colt, Calvin Wolter, Nural Bekiroglu, David Camann, Patricia Hartge, and John R. Nuckols. 2006. "Proximity to Crops and Residential Exposure to Agricultural Herbicides in Iowa." *Environmental Health Perspectives* 114 (6): 893–897. <doi.org/10.1289/ehp.8770>

Wheeler, P. A., and R. B. Ward. 2006. *The Non-Toxic Farming Handbook.* Austin: Acres USA.

Wilmers, C. C., R. L. Crabtree, D. W. Smith, K. M. Murphy, and W. M. Getz. 2003. "Trophic Facilitation by Introduced Top Predators: Grey Wolf Subsidies to Scavengers in Yellowstone National Park." *Journal of Animal Ecology* 72 (6): 909–916. <doi:10.1046/j.1365-2656.2003.00766.x>

Young, Jon. *Kamana Naturalist Training Program V. 3.0.* Duvall: Taweya Productions, 1996.

Acknowledgments

There are so many people who influenced this book, and one in particular has stood beside me and given me the support and courage to write this story: my husband, Erik Markegard. He helped care for the kids and the ranches especially during the early mornings. I love you. I owe an equal acknowledgement to Suzanna Hall, who, with a gracious smile, picked up the slack, which was not always easy and often meant long days of hard work and exhaustion. Endless hugs and kisses to my children, Lea, Larry, Quill, and Quince, whose patience and excitement about my writing got me through.

Katy Bowman, thank you for believing in me and having the inspiration to follow through on your instinct and contact me to write this. And to all the staff at Propriometrics Press, it has been a pleasure to work with you. To my editor, Penelope Jackson, thank you for immersing in this story and keeping the message while asking me the difficult questions that pushed me to soar to new heights. Caroline Tracey, I admire your writing skills and I am indebted to your support with the works cited.

I would like to thank all of the mentors and students during my time at Wilderness Awareness School and the trackers I have worked with: Gilbert Walking Bull, Jon Young, Tom Brown Jr., Paul Rezendes, Louis Liebenberg, Mark Elbroch,

James Halfpenny, Ingwe (Norman Powell), Jake Swamp, Macki Ruka, Anne Osbaldeston, Warren Moon, Justin Alexander, Greg Sommer, Terry Crane, Chris Laliberte, Rikki Scandora Tyler, Rhiannon Kreal, Vijay Lih, Becca Hall, Aidan Young, Josh Sommer, Yssa Hill, Patricia and Sabah Baird, Amber Zandanel, Michael Doran, Bobbe Branch, Jake Jacobson, Jenn Wolfe, Dan Gardoqui, Nate Summers and John Gallagher. Thank you Tony Ten Fingers, who reviewed all of the Lakota language for me (all errors, however, are my own).

` Thank you to my family—my big sisters, Serene and Chantal, my mother, Miriam, and all of my extended family who have believed in me. To my grammy, whose homestead stories added depth to my own history. Thank you to all the Women in Ranching for your support.

Allan Savory, thank you for your work, which has inspired so many in the field of Holistic Management.

Thank you to the supporters of this story: Joel Salatin, Judith Schwartz, Tristan Gooley, Courtney White, Charles Massy, Stephanie Anderson, and Michelle Roehm McCann. Thank you to all of the youth who mobilized for the 2019 Youth Climate strikes across the globe. I hear you and am taking action to address this crisis.

About the Author

Doniga Markegard is a wildlife tracker, regenerative rancher, speaker, and author. Her teen years in nature school started her on a path that led to a career in animal tracking and then permaculture and ranching in California, where she works to regenerate both soil and community through farming. Using the innovative, carbon-storing methods of regenerative ranching, she's restoring the land she tends, bringing native grasses and wildlife back to the depleted Bay Area. Doniga is a consultant and guest instructor at numerous nature and permaculture programs around the country and is a regular speaker at events such as the Bioneers Conference, Food Inspiration Trendsummit, and The Grassfed Exchange; has worked with companies such as Patagonia and Google; and has been featured in articles from *Fast Company*, *GreenBiz*, *The San Francisco Examiner*, and NPR.